What is Iran?

What is Iran?
A Primer on Culture, Politics and Religion

Commissioned by Mennonite Central Committee

Laurie Blanton Pierce

Herald Press

Scottdale, Pennsylvania
Waterloo, Ontario

A shepherd grazes his sheep in the semi-arid landscape of the Zagros Mountains, near Shiraz.

On the cover: A young Iranian woman converses with members of an MCC learning tour in the midst of Ashura processions outside the main shrine in Qom. Photo by Jon Rudy, 2006.

Acknowledgments

I would like to thank Matthew Pierce, Ata Anzali, Daryl Byler, Yousef Daneshvar, Susan Harrison, Scott Harrop, Jan Martens Janzen, Rick Janzen, Haydeh Javandel, Hajj Muhammad Legenhausen, Ed Martin, Don Peters, Evelyn Shellenberger, Wallace Shellenberger, Hendrick Shenazarian, Gladys Terichow, and Sonia K. Weaver for their advice, support, and contributions. I would also like to express my gratitude to the many people of Iran, Canada, the United States, and elsewhere who have supported and participated in the MCC-IKERI exchange program. The rewards of friendships formed through this program are more than I can number.

Library of Congress Cataloging-in-Publication Data

Pierce, Laurie Blanton.
  What is Iran? : a primer on culture, politics, and religion / by
Laurie Blanton Pierce ; commissioned by Mennonite Central Committee.
  p. cm.
  Includes bibliographical references and index.
  ISBN 978-0-8361-9446-3 (pbk. : alk. paper)
  1. Iran—Politics and government—1979-1997. 2. Iran—Politics and
government—1997- I. Mennonite Central Committee. II. Title.
  DS318.825.P54 2009
  955.05'4—dc22

                                                    2009002882

WHAT IS IRAN?
Copyright © 2009 by Herald Press,
Scottdale, Pa. 15683
    Published simultaneously in Canada by Herald Press, Waterloo, Ont. N2L 6H7.
    All rights reserved
Library of Congress Catalog Card Number: 2009002882
International Standard Book Number: 978-0-8361-9446-3
Printed in Canada
Design by Juliana Fast
Photos by Mark Beach, Ron Dueck, Ron Flaming, Elizabeth Holdeman, Doug Hostetter, Linda Kusse, Hajj Muhammad Legenhausen, William Miller, Janet Pierce, Laurie Pierce, Matthew Pierce, Jon Rudy, David Wolfe, and others.
All passages from the Qur'an on pp. 16, 87, were taken from the Penguin Classics Version, translated by N. J. Dawood.

14 13 12 11 10 09 10 9 8 7 6 5 4 3 2 1

To order or request information please call
1-800-245-7894 or visit www.heraldpress.com

A wintry scene at ex-shah's palace, Tehran.

Table of Contents

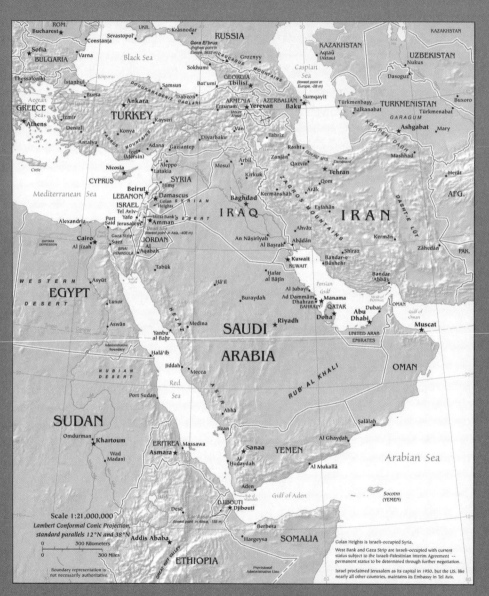

Map of Iran and surrounding countries from CIA World Factbook.

The Tehran skyline at sunrise.

Introduction

Carving on the eastern entrance of the Gate of All Nations at Persepolis. The ruins of Persepolis, which served as the ceremonial capital of the Persian Empire during the Achaemenid dynasty, date back some 2,500 years.

Introduction

Mennonite Central Committee (MCC) is the relief, development, and peace committee of the Mennonite and Brethren in Christ churches in Canada and the United States. It seeks to demonstrate God's love by working among suffering people; striving for peace, justice, and the dignity of all people; and serving as a channel for interchange by building mutually transformative relationships.

In the early 1990s MCC partnered with the Iranian Red Crescent Society to provide relief to victims of a devastating earthquake in northern Iran. MCC involvement in the country later expanded to include a Christian-Muslim exchange program, and I studied in Iran as part of that program from 2003 to 2006. During that time I experienced first-hand the kind of mutually transformative relationships that MCC seeks to build. Such relationships depend on understanding, and this book has emerged from MCC's commitment to cultivating understanding between Mennonite Christians and Shi'a Muslims. *What is Iran?* follows in the footsteps of *What is Palestine-Israel?*, a book by Sonia K. Weaver that provides an overview of the Palestinian-Israeli conflict rooted in MCC experience in the region.

The first three chapters of this book are designed to provide readers with some of the information necessary for a basic understanding of contemporary Iran. Chapter 1 outlines the ethnic and religious makeup of Iranian society, with a focus on Shi'a Islam. Chapters 2 and 3 give an overview of Iranian political history from the nineteenth century to the present, with emphasis on events leading to the Islamic Revolution of 1979 and a discussion of the changes in Iranian society since the Revolution. The fourth chapter of the book touches on key issues in present-day Iranian-Western political relations and seeks to answer questions Mennonites in North America have asked MCC service workers returning from Iran. The book's fifth chapter deals with Anabaptist responses to

Iran, including a summary of Anabaptist involvement in the country, suggestions on helpful ways of thinking about Iran, and ways in which we can work toward peaceful relations with Iran and Iranians.

A short book such as this can never provide readers with a complete description or understanding of an entire country, least of all a country with as long a history and complex a society as Iran's. Because this book is written for people in Canada and the United States, it primarily discusses the aspects of Iranian history, politics, and society that tend to interest that audience. Western interest in Iran is greatly shaped by news media accounts, which in recent decades have dealt mainly with contentious political issues such as Iran's nuclear program, human rights record, and its leaders' statements about Israel. These topics and others addressed in the book are incredibly complex, and such a brief treatment necessarily involves simplification and generalization. In addition, while these issues are significant, it is important to remember that Iranian society, culture, and history extend far beyond them, and that many important events in Iranian history and aspects of Iranian society and culture have been left out.

While writing this book I happened upon an article in *The New Yorker* (August 20, 2007, pp. 2, 29) called "The Dark Side," by David Owen. The article talks of how air and light pollution have greatly eroded our view of the heavens, with the result that a person standing atop the Empire State Building and looking skyward on a clear night will see only 1 percent of the wonders that were visible to Galileo's naked eye some four centuries ago. With this in mind, a group called the International Dark-Sky Association (IDA) is working to cut down the pollutions that obstruct our view of the stars. The members of the IDA, writes Owen, are scattered across the globe, with some living in Iraq and Iran, "where astronomy is a popular hobby, especially among girls and young women." Owen goes on to say that "Authorities in Sa'adat-shahr, about four hundred miles south of Tehran, periodically cut off all electric power in the town in order to improve visibility at nighttime 'star parties' conducted by a local teacher." I was delighted to find a reference to Iran in a mainstream publication that wasn't accompanied by a mention of the nuclear issue or Iranian President Mahmoud Ahmadinejad's remarks on the Holocaust, and despite having met a number of people interested in astronomy while I was in Iran, I was surprised that an entire town was willing to go without electricity so that students could stargaze.

Iran still has the power to surprise us here in the West, even thirty years after the country's 1979 revolution came as such a shock to so many. We may be taken aback by the enthusiasm of Sa'adat-shahr's inhabitants for

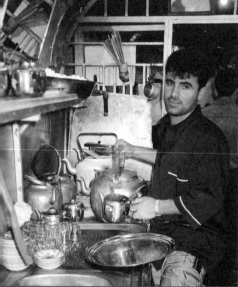

Top: An instrument maker at work in a shop at the Haft Tanan Museum and Garden in Shiraz.

Bottom: A man makes tea at a shop under a bridge.

astronomy—an enthusiasm that sparked women to give their jewelry and civil servants give a portion of their salaries to help build the town's impressive observatory. We might also be surprised that Iran produces world-class films, that women make up over 60 percent of its university students, and that the country has some of the best literacy and healthcare statistics in the region. Sadly, what might surprise many people the most is that life in Iran isn't really surprising after all. Iranians get up every morning and go to school; work; and religious, social, and business gatherings. They find joy and sorrow in family relationships and friendships, hope to advance in their careers, worry about their children's education and future, find themselves concerned by the current events that make the news, and turn to religious faith for meaning and guidance in life. In short, Iranians' lives look a lot like our own.

This book is designed to provide answers to some of the common questions people in Canada and the United States have about Iran. I hope that it will also prompt readers to turn out the lights of the media and look beyond talked-about current events to learn about the many aspects of Iran that don't make the news. The resources section at the end of the book is a starting point for those who wish to delve more deeply into topics related to Iran.

My interest in Islam and the peoples and cultures of the Muslim world predates my time in Iran. As an adolescent I moved with my family to Peshawar, Pakistan, where my father worked for a humanitarian aid organization. Later, after attending college in the United States, my husband and I worked and studied in Egypt and then Yemen before beginning the MCC student exchange in Iran. My experience in these countries has been formative, and the friends I have found in each place have shaped my perspective and my faith. It is my hope that this book offers not only information about Iran, but also a glimpse of the life-enriching possibility of friendships formed across political, religious, and cultural boundaries.

—*Laurie Blanton Pierce, Boston, Massachusetts*

A group of men sitting outside a highway rest stop.

The Faces and Faiths of Iran

Ethnic Breakdown of Iran's Peoples

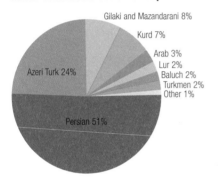

Gilaki and Mazandarani 8%
Kurd 7%
Arab 3%
Lur 2%
Baluch 2%
Turkmen 2%
Other 1%
Azeri Turk 24%
Persian 51%

Religious Breakdown of Iran's Peoples

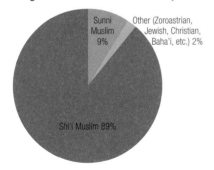

Sunni Muslim 9%
Other (Zoroastrian, Jewish, Christian, Baha'i, etc.) 2%
Shi'i Muslim 89%

Information from CIA World Factbook.

1. The Faces and Faiths of Iran

The modern nation state of Iran is the direct descendant of the Persian Empire and as such has an extremely rich and prestigious cultural heritage. Following the mainly peaceful Islamic conquest of Persia in the seventh century, the face of Persian society was changed, but many fundamental elements of Persian culture were retained and went on to influence the development and practice of Islam in Persia and beyond. Iran acquired its distinctly Shi'a character under the Safavid dynasty (1502-1722), which declared Twelver Shi'a Islam, the largest branch of Shi'a Islam, the state religion of the country. In many ways Shi'a Islam and Persian history, language, and culture can be considered defining characteristics of Iran, but it is important to remember that the country's seventy million inhabitants belong to a great number of ethnic groups, speak many different languages and dialects, follow a variety of lifestyles, and adhere to different religions.

I. The Ethnic Landscape of Iranian Society

Around half of Iranians are ethnic Persians, and their native Farsi (also called Persian) is the primary language of the country. Azeri Turks, who speak a variety of Turkic languages and dialects, make up around one quarter of the population and are a significant part of the cultural landscape of Iran. The remaining quarter of Iranian society is made up primarily of minorities concentrated in the border regions, including the Gilaki and Mazandarani peoples south of the Caspian Sea, Arabs in the southwest, Kurds in the northwest, as well as smaller populations of Turkmen in the northeast, Baluch in the southeast and Lur in the west.

II. The Religious Landscape of Iranian Society

Iran's religious landscape is significantly less diverse than its ethnic and linguistic landscapes. Nearly 90 percent of the population is Shi'a Muslim, and Shi'a Islamic identity is a significant unifying force within Iranian society. An additional 8 or 9 percent of Iranians are Sunni Muslim, and the remaining 2 percent of the country's population is divided among minority religions including Christianity, Judaism, Zoroastrianism, and the Baha'i faith.

ISLAM

The word *Islam* means "submission," and in its most basic form Islam is the submission of all creation to the will of God. The word is also used more specifically in reference to the conscious attempt by human beings to live in harmony with God's will. In its most specific sense, the term is used for the religion instituted by the mission of the prophet Muhammad. As a religion, Islam, like Christianity, has a long and complex history that encompasses a huge array of beliefs and practices. Muslims belong to a wide variety of Islamic sects and adhere to nearly every conceivable political, social, and religious ideology. Because Islam is lived out in so many different places and cultural contexts, and because Muslims disagree about some aspects of their religion, it can be misleading to speak in generalities about Islam. Nonetheless, a set of beliefs and practices lies at the core of the faith and is shared by nearly all the world's Muslims. Knowledge of these core elements is helpful in understanding the religion that shapes Iranian society.

Core Beliefs

• **The Unity of God** — The concept of the oneness of God is central to Islam, and Muslims ascribe to a strictly monotheistic concept of God (also called *Allah*, which is simply the Arabic word for God). The conception of God as trinity tends to be one

Islamic Spirituality

The inner, or mystical, dimension of Islam is commonly called Sufism. Sufism is concerned with the Islamic concept of "doing what is beautiful," and the essence of Sufi practice is overcoming one's worldly desires and attachments in order to surrender the self to loving God. The goal of this self-surrender is for the believer to fully experience—to the point of being consumed by—the presence and love of God.

Sufism has existed in a variety of forms since the early days of Islam, and to this day the tales of famous Sufis, or mystics, inform the spirituality of many Muslims. One of the most famous mystics in Islam is Rabi'a, who is said to have knelt a thousand times per day and said "I ask for nothing but to satisfy the Almighty God." She is also said to have walked the paths of her village holding a pail of water in one hand and a torch aloft in the other. When asked why, Rabi'a remarked that she wished to extinguish the flames of hell with the water and to enflame heaven with the torch, so that people would worship God not from fear of hell or desire for heaven, but out of love.

Iran is home to a number of Sufi orders, and Sufism has greatly influenced Iranian literary culture and Shi'a philosophy. Sufism and Sufi poetry have also become popular in the West. Some Muslims have criticized radical forms of Sufism as "un-Islamic," noting that some Sufis have gone to extremes of asceticism or have failed to perform basic Islamic practices. Additionally, many Shi'a differentiate between orthodox Islamic spirituality and the sometimes heterodox beliefs and practices of Sufi orders and individuals.

SELECTIONS FROM THE QUR'AN

The Fatiha

The following is a translation of the opening chapter (*sura*) of the Qur'an, which serves as the most frequently recited prayer in Islam.

In the Name of God the Compassionate the Merciful
Praise be to God, Lord of the Universe,
The Compassionate, the Merciful,
Sovereign of the Day of Judgment!
You alone we worship, and to You alone
We turn for help.
Guide us to the straight path,
The path of those whom You have favoured,
Not of those who have incurred Your wrath,
Nor of those who have gone astray.

Sura al-Nur, Verse 35

The following is a translation of a verse from the *sura* known as "Light."

God is the light of the heavens and the earth. His light may be compared to a niche that enshrines a lamp, the lamp within a crystal of star-like brilliance. It is lit from a blessed olive tree neither eastern nor western. Its very oil would almost shine forth, though no fire touched it. Light upon light; God guides to His light whom He will.

of the most problematic aspects of Christianity for Muslims, for the Qur'an clearly states that "God is One, the Eternal God. He begot none, nor was He begotten. None is equal to Him." (112:1-4)

• **Divine Guidance: Prophethood, the Qur'an, and the *Sunnah*** — Muslims believe that God sent many prophets to bring divine guidance for humanity, including Noah, Abraham, Moses, Jesus, and Muhammad, who is considered the final prophet. They believe that God revealed books to some of these prophets, including the Qur'an, which Muslims believe was revealed word for word in 114 chapters (*suras*) to Prophet Muhammad over the course of his life. The Qur'an is highly praised for its literary beauty and is by far the most important source of Islamic law, belief and practice. Another important source in Islam is the *Sunnah*—an Arabic word meaning "way" or "path." In the context of Islamic doctrine it refers to the way the Prophet Muhammad lived his life. The *Sunnah* is derived from various collections of *hadiths*, or narrations about what the Prophet said and did. While the Qur'an is considered the inerrant word of God, collections of *hadiths* are believed in some cases to include dubious narrations.

• **Resurrection and the Day of Judgment** — Like Christians, Muslims believe that the world as we know it will come to an end when all will be brought before God to be judged in accordance with divine justice and mercy.

Core Practices

Five religious practices, or the "Five Pillars," as they are commonly known, form the backbone of religious observance for Muslims worldwide.

• **Bearing Witness** — The first of these pillars is the creed which states "There is no deity but God, and Muhammad is the messenger of God." This statement is Islamic doctrine in a nutshell, and saying it with sincerity makes one a Muslim.

• **Ritual Prayer** — Ritual prayers are performed five times per day, and this rhythm of prayer shapes the spiritual life of practicing Muslims.

• **Almsgiving** — Islam requires that Muslims give a certain percentage of their annual income to help the poor and to benefit society.

• **Fasting** — Muslims fast from sun-up to sundown on each of the days of the Islamic month of Ramadan. In Islamic countries Ramadan is often the most festive month of the year and a time when the community comes together in hospitality and friendship.

• **Hajj (Pilgrimage)** — All Muslims who are physically and financially able are required to go on pilgrimage to Mecca once in their lifetime. Many who go on this pilgrimage cite hajj as the best and most memorable experience of their lives.

Shi'a Islam and Iran

The two major divisions of Islam are Sunni and Shi'a, with approximately 85 percent of the world's Muslims being Sunni, and the remaining 15 percent Shi'a. The Sunni-Shi'a split arose immediately after the death of the prophet Muhammad in a dispute over the leadership of the Muslim community. The Sunni believe that the succession of the prophet should be decided by the leaders of the community. Meanwhile, the Shi'a believe that it is a matter of divine appointment, and that Muhammad announced this appointment in a public ceremony at which his followers were invited to pledge allegiance to the leadership (Imamate) of his nephew Ali, through whom divine guidance would continue to be provided for the community. The Shi'a believe that with the death of Muhammad the cycle of prophethood ended and the cycle of Imamate began. So, in addition to the core beliefs they share with other Muslims, the Shi'a add a belief in the Imamate. The majority of the world's Shi'a (including the vast majority of

SELECTION FROM THE *SUNNAH*

The *Hadith* of Gabriel
Long regarded by Muslim scholars as a summary of the foundational beliefs and practices of Islam, this *hadith* was narrated by one of the close companions of Prophet Muhammad and tells of a time when the angel Gabriel appeared to the Prophet and spoke the following:

... *"Submission means that you should bear witness that there is no god but God and that Muhammad is God's messenger, that you should perform the ritual prayer, pay the alms tax, fast during Ramadan, and make the pilgrimage to the House if you are able to go there."* ...

... *"Faith means that you have faith in God, His angels, His books, His messengers, and the Last Day, and that you have faith in the measuring out, both its good and its evil."* ...

... *"Doing what is beautiful means that you should worship God as if you see Him, for even if you do not see Him, He sees you."* ...

—translated from the Arabic by William Chittick

"The duty that seems most important for the Muslim's daily life and which has shaped the Islamic world most strongly is the second pillar, ritual prayer." *–Annemarie Schimmel*

In contrast to Sunni Muslims, who followed a line of caliphs after Prophet Muhammad's death until the fall of the Ottoman Empire in 1923, Shi'a Muslims followed a line of direct descendants of the Prophet. Twelver Shi'a recognize twelve of these imams, who are called, along with Prophet Muhammad and his daughter Fatima, the "Fourteen Infallibles."

Ali ibn Abi Talib (The son-in-law and close associate of Prophet Muhammad)

Hassan ibn Ali (Elder son of Ali and grandson of the Prophet)

Hussein ibn Ali (Younger brother of Hassan, martyred at Karbala and greatly revered)

Ali ibn Hussein (Also known as Zayn al-Abedin, "Jewel of the Believers")

Muhammad ibn Ali (Also known as Al-Baqir, "the Revealer")

Ja'far ibn Muhammad (Also known as Al-Sadiq, "the Truthful;" holds an important place in Shi'a jurisprudence)

Musa ibn Ja'far (Also known as Al-Kazem, "the Peaceful")

Ali ibn Musa (Also known as Al-Reza, "the Pleasing;" his shrine in Mashhad, Iran is visited by millions of pilgrims each year)

Muhammad ibn Ali (Also known as Al-Javad, "the Generous")

Ali ibn Muhammad (Also known as Al-Hadi, "the Leader")

Hassan ibn Ali (Also known as Al-Askari, in reference to his being held in a military prison for much of his life)

Muhammad ibn Hassan (also known as Al-Mahdi, the final imam who will return at the end of the world)

Iran's Shi'a) are called Twelver, or Imami, Shi'a, because they followed a line of twelve imams (leaders) beginning with Imam Ali and ending with Imam Mahdi. The imams are said to have provided divine guidance, but unlike the prophets, they do not bring a new revealed book or a new divine law. Shi'a believe that the final imam did not die, but rather went into hiding to reappear together with Jesus at the time of his second coming.

• **Shi'a Practices** — In many ways the religious lives of Iranian Shi'a are similar to those of their Sunni coreligionists, but practices and beliefs unique to Shi'a Islam influence the way they observe their faith. One of these practices is the commemoration of the death of Imam Hussein. Hussein was the grandson of the prophet Muhammad and the third imam of Shi'a Islam. In the year 680, Hussein and about seventy of his followers, along with their wives and children, were attacked in the desert by forces of the Umayyad Caliph Yazid, who perceived Hussein as a threat to his rule. Outnumbered by the thousands, Hussein and his followers were killed and the women and children in their party taken captive. The story of Hussein's martyrdom is a formative element in Shi'a Islam, and it serves as a symbol of the struggle against tyranny and injustice. Hussein was killed on the tenth day of the Islamic month of Muharram, known as Ashura. Muharram is a unique time in Iran when Shi'a Muslims gather together to mourn and hear preaching inspired by the stories of the martyrs. Mourning ceremonies reach their peak on Ashura, when crowds of the faithful proceed through the streets in public displays of grief that involve weeping, reciting prayers, chanting, and striking their chests rhythmically with their hands. Some mourners flagellate themselves with chains, but religious authorities condemn excesses and any injury to oneself as incongruent with Islamic teaching.

Another practice of great importance to Iran's Shi'a Muslims is visiting the shrines of Shi'a Imams and other important religious figures. A visit can involve a short trip to a local gravesite; travel to another city; or a cross-border trek to revered shrines in Karbala and Najaf, Iraq, and in Damascus, Syria. Shi'a visit these shrines as an expression of their devotion to the Imams and all of the family of the prophet Muhammad and to seek the intercession of the saints with God on their behalf. A visit to a shrine involves prayer and monetary offerings and is often an emotionally moving experience for the believer. The most important shrines in Iran are the shrine of Imam Ali Reza in Mashhad and the shrine of his sister Lady Fatima Ma'suma in Qom, which are visited by millions of pilgrims each year.

• **Shi'a Religious Authority** — For a variety of historical reasons the Shi'a clergy today tend to have more influence in their own community than do their Sunni counterparts. Shi'a clergy are trained in seminaries in a variety of cities across the Muslim world with Qom, Iran, and Najaf, Iraq, being the two greatest centers of Shi'a learning. There are many different levels of clergy, and rising to the rank of top religious leader requires great aptitude and a lifetime of learning. Each Shi'a lay person chooses a leading member of the clergy (known as a "source of emulation") to follow and bases his or her religious life on that leader's interpretation of Islamic law. The presence of a number of religious leaders with equal qualifications and status but varying interpretations of Islam allows diverse points of view to coexist and flourish within Shi'a Islam. For example, top religious leaders will often differ in their views on broad topics such as the role of religion in government, modern economics, and interfaith relations as well as on smaller points of Islamic law.

Sunni Islam in Iran

Prior to the Safavid dynasty, under which Shi'a Islam flourished and spread, Iran was predominantly a Sunni country. Today, however, Sunni Muslims make up about 9 percent of the

Shi'a Pilgrimage

An Iranian Shi'a Muslim tells the story of his journey to the shrine of Imam Reza.

Every day the Iranian city of Mashhad is host to tens of thousands of pilgrims who come to visit the tomb of the eighth imam. While most pilgrims use modern transportation to reach the shrine, my friends and I made the pilgrimage on foot.

It was one of the most inspiring and exciting experiences of my life. We walked long hours in sweltering temperatures. The first few days were disappointing as our bodies struggled to adapt, and the heat left us barely able to breathe. After a couple of days, however, I realized something was happening inside me. I felt a new source of vitality welling up like a cold spring finding its way through hard rocks. A vast space opened in my heart, and my eyes opened to the realm of the sacred.

Externally, my two hundred fellow pilgrims and I walked together, laughing, eating, and cursing the tractor trailer trucks that thundered by on the road, shaking us in their wake. But internally, as we gazed into the infinite spaces of naked desert that surrounded us, our souls flourished in the sacred solitude of contemplation. For the first time I understood the mentality of wandering Sufis at the dawn of Islam; they belonged nowhere, and so the whole earth was their home. Maybe this is the same non-attachment Buddhist monks talk about.

We had expected the journey to culminate in our physical visit to the shrine, but we soon realized that the rules of the realm of the spirit, where our souls travel, are quite different. There, the distance between the beginning and the end, between yesterday and tomorrow, is less important, more blurred. There, the journey itself is the blessing.

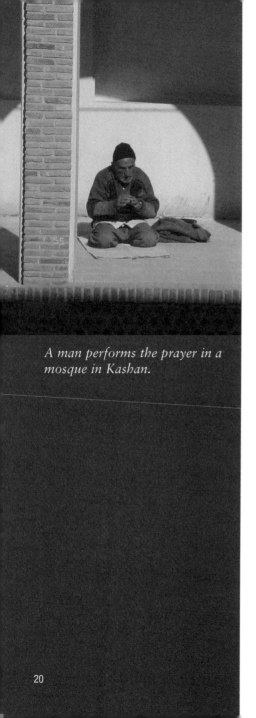

A man performs the prayer in a mosque in Kashan.

population and are mainly non-Persian peoples living in the border areas of Iran, specifically the Baluch of the southeast, Kurds and Arabs of the north and southwest, and the Turkmen of the northeast. The Iranian constitution, while enshrining Twelver Shi'a Islam as the state religion of Iran, guarantees Sunni Muslims the right to practice according to their interpretations of the faith and allows them full participation in government with a few exceptions. One of these exceptions is that Sunni Muslims are not eligible to run for president. Senior members of the Shi'a clergy and prominent government officials have repeatedly called for Sunni-Shi'a unity and tolerance. Sunni communities, however, have complaints regarding under-representation in local and national government as well as the low quality of services and infrastructure in the outlying regions of the country, which negatively affect both the majority Sunni and the minority Shi'a in these areas. Sunnis have also cited government-imposed restrictions on their freedom of worship, most notably the refusal of the government to grant the one-million strong Sunni community of Tehran a permit to build a mosque. In many cases such problems pre-exist the revolutionary government, and it is often unclear whether complaints are rooted in religious or ethnic discrimination. In addition, government fear of minority groups' connections with separatists and opposition groups both inside and outside the country plays a role in the treatment of these communities.

MINORITY RELIGIONS IN IRAN

The government of Iran recognizes three minority religions: Christianity, Judaism, and Zoroastrianism. These religions have long and distinguished histories in the country, and peaceful (if not problem-free) coexistence with the Muslim majority has been the norm for significant periods of those histories. The ideal of religious tolerance has long been a part of the Persian ethos, and the idea that monotheists of pre-Islamic faiths—that "people of the book," the name given to Jews, Christians, and other faith groups in the Qur'an—should be treated with respect and fairness, is rooted in the doctrines of Islam. The present Islamic government in Iran, however, is often criticized by the international community for discrimination against religious minorities. When evaluating these critiques, it is necessary to recognize that the government of Iran does espouse a vision of religious rights, though this vision differs from dominant conceptions of human rights in western societies.

Under the Iranian constitution, minority faith communities have the right to practice their beliefs within the limits of the law. This includes a great deal of freedom in the areas of education and religious and cultural expression, though such freedom is often compromised by close government scrutiny and practices such as the appointing of Muslim headmasters to oversee minority schools. Christian, Jewish, and Zoroastrian communities are guaranteed parliamentary representation, with two seats reserved for Armenian Christians, one seat for Assyrian and Chaldean Christians, and one each for the Jewish and Zoroastrian communities. Advocates of this system point out that the percentage of minority seats in parliament is greater than the percentage of minorities in Iranian society, but others are troubled by the fact that members of religious minorities are ineligible to run for most other high-level government posts. The Iranian government allocates money for the restoration and upkeep of Jewish and Christian buildings, and recognized religious minorities have legal jurisdiction over their own communities in some matters such as marriage, divorce, and inheritance law. Nonetheless, both recognized and unrecognized minority communities in Iran complain of institutionalized discrimination in the penal code of Iran, which in some cases treats Muslims and non-Muslims differently.

Minority communities experienced serious erosions in their rights following the revolution of 1979, but advances were made in the 1990s and beyond. In the past several years, however, the

Religious Tolerance in Persian Poetry

The most famous example of ecumenical spirit in Persian poetry can be found in the writings of the Sufi poet Hatef Esfahani, who lived in the eighteenth century. Esfahani is best known for a poem containing the message that Muslims, Zoroastrians, and Christians all worship the same God. The poem begins with an invocation of God that is common in Persian mystical literature:

"O Thou to whom both heart and life are a sacrifice, and O Thou in whose path both this and that are an offering!

"The heart is Thy sacrifice because Thou art a charmer of hearts; life is Thine offering because Thou art the Life of our lives."

The poet then tells of going to a Zoroastrian temple, where he is hailed as a "lover," which in mystical poetry symbolizes a person who seeks union with God. He also goes to a church, where he asks a Christian woman why she believes in the trinity. She gives a beautiful, symbolic explanation of the trinity and goes on to affirm the oneness of God. Later the poet visits a tavern, where he finds the drinkers rapt in contemplation of the divine (in Persian poetry, wine and drunkenness serve as metaphors of ecstatic religious experience). Esfahani concludes each stanza with a refrain containing the central message of the poem, which is spoken by all who love God regardless of creed:

"He is One and there is naught but He: There is no God save Him alone!"

—*A Literary History of Persia*, Vol. IV, by Edward G. Browne, Iranbooks

NOTABLE CHURCHES OF IRAN

Iran is home to a number of beautiful and historic churches and monasteries. Some of these sites date back to the earliest days of Christianity, but most were built in the seventeenth century by Armenian Orthodox Christians who came to Iran from Armenia and Azerbaijan. The city of Esfahan and the provinces of East and West Azerbaijan are home to the largest concentrations of churches in Iran, though notable structures exist in other cities and provinces as well. The following rank among the country's most remarkable Christian edifices.

Vank Cathedral

A monastery was built on this site in the Christian quarter of Esfahan known as New Jolfa in the early seventeenth century, shortly after the arrival of Armenians in the city. The present structure dates back to the late seventeenth century and is ornamented by a variety of striking paintings depicting various scenes from the Old and New Testaments. The cathedral grounds are also home to a library and museum housing Armenian books and artifacts and a monument commemorating the Armenian holocaust.

situation of religious minorities, particularly that of the Baha'i, has deteriorated. High rates of emigration abroad among adherents to minority faiths, especially Christianity and Judaism, have also been a concern of those communities. Such emigration is partially prompted by the inequities listed above, but general economic conditions in Iran are at least as big, if not a bigger, factor in prompting members of religious minorities to leave Iran.

Christianity in Iran

Christians have been present in Iran since the earliest days of the faith, and estimates of the number of Christians in Iran today range from one hundred thousand to three hundred thousand. Most of Iran's Christians are ethnically Armenian and belong to the Armenian Orthodox Apostolic Church. The Armenian Orthodox Church is an autonomous branch of Eastern Christianity that traces its origins to the preaching of disciples of Christ in the first century. Armenian Orthodoxy was adopted as the official religion of the kingdom of Armenia at the beginning of the fourth century, marking the first time Christianity was named a state religion. Armenians and Persians have a history of interaction that predates the advent of both Christianity and Islam, and much of the Armenian community of today's Iran has its roots in an early seventeenth-century migration in which large numbers of Armenians were removed from their lands by the Safavid Shah Abbas I and resettled in Esfahan, where they flourished in commerce and industry. The situation of the Armenian Christian community in Iran fluctuated according to the attitude of the kings of subsequent dynasties. The Armenian Christians of today's Iran live mainly in Tehran and Esfahan and retain their distinctively Armenian language, culture, and religious practices.

Assyrian Christians also have a long history in Iran, though they are significantly outnumbered by their Armenian counterparts. The Assyrian Church of the East split with the

Byzantine church in the fifth century as a result of the Nestorian dispute, though its doctrine today cannot properly be characterized as Nestorian. The history of the Assyrian community in Iran since that time is incredibly complex, with members of the community aligning themselves at different times with a variety of different churches. Members of Iran's Assyrian community today describe themselves as Assyrian or Chaldean and are mainly affiliated with the Assyrian Church of the East or the Chaldean Catholic Church. The Chaldean church, an offshoot of the Assyrian Church of the East, is an autonomous church in full communion with Rome. Iran's Assyrian community also includes Christians affiliated with the Assyrian Evangelical Church and the Assyrian Pentecostal Church.

As a result of Western missionary activity, Iran also has a number of Protestant and a smaller number of Roman Catholic Christians. Roman Catholic missions to Iran predate Protestant activity in the country and include the residence of the Order of the Carmelites in Esfahan under the Safavid Shah Abbas I in the sixteenth century. Protestant missionary activity in Iran began in the nineteenth century and has resulted in small Iranian mainline Protestant and evangelical churches whose numbers are difficult to establish because they are not recognized by the Iranian government. Western missionary activity has historically been regarded with great suspicion by Iranians and their governments, partially due to Islamic prohibitions concerning the conversion of Muslims to other religions, but more specifically because such missionary efforts have often been tied to foreign governments hostile to Iranian sovereignty. Indigenous Iranian Christians have also viewed missionary activity with suspicion, in part because Western missionaries have sometimes aimed their conversion efforts at members of the traditional churches, and partly because connection with Western Christianity has tended to jeopardize the already-tenuous position of Christians in a greater Iranian society that has long distrusted Western influence and power.

The Church of St. Thaddeus

Christian construction on this site near Maku in the northwestern tip of Iran dates back to the fourth century, possibly even earlier. A church built in the seventh century was destroyed by an earthquake in the early fourteenth century and then rebuilt several decades later. Other parts were added as centuries passed, including those portions built of black stone from which the church gets its other name, *Qareh Kelisa* (the Black Church). In June of each year, Christian pilgrims come from all over Iran to camp in the plains around the church and celebrate the feast day of St. Thaddeus.

The Monastery of St. Stephen

This striking church is tucked among the hills of the remote border regions of northwest Iran. A church is said to have been built at this site by St. Bartholomew in the first century, and parts of the current structure date back to the fourteenth century.

Protestant and evangelical churches, particularly those unrecognized by the Islamic Republic, tend to have far more numerous and broad-ranging complaints of discrimination than the recognized indigenous churches. The Iranian government, for a variety of historical reasons, is deeply suspicious of Christian groups originating in or having connections to the West. The fact that some of these groups' members are converts from Islam puts these churches further at odds with the Islamic state, which outlaws proselytization by non-Islamic groups. Protestant and evangelical churches have cited frequent harassment by government officials and have experienced arrests and mysterious deaths of church leaders and members.

Judaism in Iran

The history of Judaism in Iran dates back thousands of years to the Babylonian exile in the sixth century BCE, and the Persian Jewish community has maintained its presence in the country throughout the changes brought by the Islamic conquest and subsequent dynasties and governments of Iran. Today Iran's Jews, who number between twenty thousand and thirty thousand, make up the largest Middle Eastern Jewish community outside of Israel. The situation of Jews in relation to greater Iranian society has fluctuated over the centuries and been affected by the tension between Islam's recognition of Judaism as a divine religion on one hand, and the popular prejudice of majority communities against Jews on the other. From the sixteenth to the nineteenth centuries, Jews often faced severe discrimination similar to that faced by their coreligionists in Europe of the same time period. The Pahlavi era (1925–1979) had a mixed record of its treatment of the Iranian Jewish community.

Following the formation of the state of Israel in 1948, large numbers of Iranian Jews emigrated to Israel. The 1979 revolution prompted further emigration of the Jewish community to the West despite an order by Khomeini that the Jewish minority be protected. Tension between Iran and Israel and the United States at times puts today's Iranian Jews in a tenuous situation. Anti-Semitic acts in Iran are relatively rare, but several such incidents occurred following the 2000 conviction of ten Iranian Jews from Shiraz on charges of illegal connections to Israel. Many of the charges were later overturned, and all those convicted have since been released. Moris Motamed, former occupant of the Jewish seat in the Iranian parliament and prominent member of the Iranian Jewish community, stresses the loyalty of that community to its home country. He has, however, expressed concern over anti-Semitic trends in Iranian broadcasting as well as the remarks of Iranian President Ahmadinejad, who has publicly questioned whether the Holocaust occurred.

The Jews of Iran take pride in both their Jewish religious identity and Persian cultural heritage, and many of Iran's cities contain Jewish sites of historical note. The town of Hamadan is the site of the tombs of Esther, Mordechai, and Habakkuk. The tomb of Daniel in Shush is a popular attraction for Muslim pilgrims, and a mausoleum in Qazvin is said to house the remains of four Jewish prophets. The city of Esfahan is a treasure trove of Jewish history, with beautifully decorated synagogues and mausoleums as well as Jewish graves dating back two thousand years. The largest Jewish community in Iran today resides in Tehran, which is home to an impressive Jewish library, hospital, eleven functioning synagogues, a number of Hebrew schools, and other Jewish institutions.

Zoroastrianism in Iran

Zoroastrianism is a religion rooted in the teachings of the prophet Zoroaster (also known as Zarathustra), who lived in Persia around 1000 BCE. The religion's doctrines revolve around a monotheistic belief in a creator God known as Ahura-Mazda. Zoroastrians have typically had a dualistic view of the universe in which truth and order are pitted against falsehood and chaos.

Top: Member of the synagogue in Esfahan, preparing for Sabbath prayers.

Bottom: The interior of a synagogue in Esfahan.

The ruins of this Zoroastrian temple date back some 1,500 years and can be seen on a hilltop outside Esfahan.

Human beings play a vital role in the struggle between truth and falsehood and are urged to exercise their free will to adhere to the three basic Zoroastrian ethical principles of good thoughts, good words, and good deeds. The collection of sacred Zoroastrian texts is known as the Avesta. Fire is an important component of Zoroastrian religious ritual, serving as a symbol of the life-sustaining energy of the creator. Zoroastrianism is widely believed to have influenced Judaism, Buddhism, Christianity, and Islam.

Zoroastrianism in various forms was the official religion of several pre-Islamic Persian empires, including the Sassanian Empire, which was overthrown during the Muslim conquest of Persia in the seventh century. Following the Islamic conquest, Persians gradually converted to Islam, though a minority remained Zoroastrian through the centuries and were recognized by Muslims as "people of the book." In the early twentieth century Zoroastrians (like other Iranian religious minorities) played an active part in the Constitutional Revolution of Iran, and the Pahlavi shahs' emphasis on Iran's pre-Islamic Persian (rather than Shi'a) identity raised the status of the Zoroastrian community in Iran.

Today Zoroastrian Iranians are concentrated in Yazd, Tehran, Shiraz, Esfahan, Kerman, and Kermanshah, and some speak their own Iranian language distinct from Farsi. Zoroastrian influences can be seen in both pre-Islamic and Islamic art and architecture in Iran, and Zoroastrian temples and funeral towers can be found in many regions of the country.

The Baha'i Faith in Iran

By far the largest unrecognized religion in Iran is the Baha'i faith, which has an estimated number of three hundred thousand adherents in the country. The faith emerged in Iran in the nineteenth century from a movement known as Babism. The founder of Babism, Seyyed Ali Muhammad, proclaimed himself the Gate, or "Bab," to the twelfth Shi'a Imam Mahdi, and some say he claimed to be the Mahdi himself. The Bab attracted thousands of followers in the period between 1844 and his death in 1850, and his unorthodox teachings roused the ire of the Shi'a clerical establishment and population. Seyyed Ali Muhammad was executed in 1850, and his followers were dispersed or killed shortly after.

Approximately one decade later, Mirza Hussein Ali Nuri, a prominent early follower of the Bab, proclaimed himself to be the messianic figure whom the Bab and other religions had predicted would come. Many of the remnants of the Babi community accepted his claim and proselytized assertively on his behalf in Iran, with the result that by the 1880s nearly one hundred thousand people had converted to the new religion, known as the Baha'i faith in reference to Nuri's title "Baha'ullah."

The Baha'i community rejected some of the more aggressive Babi teachings, eschewing militancy and direct political involvement and embracing certain liberal ethical values. The Baha'i faith is monotheistic, teaching that an all-powerful, transcendent God created the universe and has been revealed to human beings throughout history via messengers known as "Manifestations of God," who bring revelation suited to the time and place in which they appear. These Manifestations of God were responsible for the founding of most world religions, which are considered valid. Divine revelation is said to be progressive, and the teachings of Baha'ullah are believed to be uniquely suited to the modern period. The religion emphasizes the value of tolerance, the equality of human beings of all races and genders, and calls for world peace and unity and the abolition of all forms of prejudice. Human beings are to respond to the messages of the Manifestations of God and worship God through obedience, prayer, and other spiritual practices and works of service.

Since the inception of their faith, Baha'is have never been well accepted in Iranian society. Initial objections to the faith were religious; Baha'is were considered apostates and their

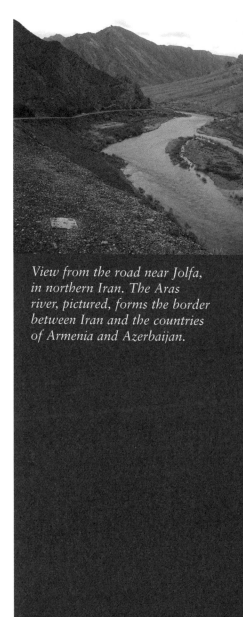

View from the road near Jolfa, in northern Iran. The Aras river, pictured, forms the border between Iran and the countries of Armenia and Azerbaijan.

A ray of sun pierces a skylight in Esfahan's Jameh Mosque.

religion heresy. Later critiques have tended to be more political in nature, with those opposed to the Baha'i citing their loyalty to unpopular Qajar and Pahlavi shahs. The location of the governing body of the Baha'i faith in Haifa, Israel, has also been a point of tension, and the Iranian government has accused Baha'is of being linked with the Israeli government. In response, Baha'is point out that their faith forbids political involvement while requiring its adherents to be obedient to the government under which they live, be it a monarchy or an Islamic republic. The Shi'a clergy have been, with a few notable exceptions, virulently anti-Baha'i, and many have encouraged the destruction of the Baha'i community with the result that a series of pogroms (organized massacres) were carried out in the 20th century, often with the tacit approval of the Qajar and Pahlavi governments.

The revolution of 1979 ushered in a period of severe repression for the Baha'i. The official position of the current Iranian government is that the Baha'i faith is not a religion but rather a subversive political movement. The practice and teaching of the Baha'i faith is illegal in Iran, and Baha'is have been subject to imprisonment and execution, particularly between 1979 and 1985. While the situation of the community has improved since that time, Baha'is who identify themselves as such continue to be denied access to employment and public higher education and subject to property confiscation and loss of inheritance rights.

Other Minority Religions

A small number of Mandaeans (or Sabeans) live along the Iraqi border and are sometimes grouped with Christians, though they do not refer to themselves in that way. Similarly, a religious group known as Ahl-e Haqq, commonly considered an offshoot of Shi'a Islam, has a number of adherents in the western province of Kermanshah. Small numbers of Hindus and adherents to various tribal religions also reside in Iran.

An Iranian couple at the entrance to Ali Qapu Palace, overlooking
Esfahan's Imam Khomeini Square and the Sheikh Lotfollah Mosque.

The Iranian
Revolution

A portrait of Ayatollah Khomeini overlooks the entrance to a building in Qom.

2. THE IRANIAN REVOLUTION

In 1978 and 1979, millions of Iranians rallied behind Ayatollah Ruhollah Khomeini and overthrew the government of Muhammad Reza Shah. Until that time, average western impressions of Iran had been formed by a media that tended to report news through a pro-shah lens, as well as by interactions with elite Iranians who were not representative of the majority of their compatriots. Thus many westerners were surprised and alarmed to see the strong anti-shah and anti-United States sentiment of revolutionary Iranians. Popular discontent with the Pahlavi monarchy and foreign powers, however, was nothing new in Iran. The seeds of the Iranian Revolution were sown decades before the events of the late 1970s, and indications that Iranians would not passively accept autocratic rule or the interference of outside powers in their country's internal affairs were apparent from the time of the Qajars, who ruled Iran from 1796 until the rise of Reza Khan, the first Pahlavi shah, in 1925.

I. Background to the Revolution

THE QAJARS AND THE TOBACCO PROTESTS

Iran entered the modern period under the Qajar dynasty (1781-1925), whose kings controlled an area that roughly corresponds with that of the modern state. The Qajar shahs were generally successful in uniting Iran under a central government, but they failed to adequately address many of the political, economic, and social challenges of their time, including the attempt by European nations to control Iran.

Throughout the nineteenth and into the twentieth century Russia and Britain were rivals for control of Central Asia in what is known as the "Great Game." This rivalry included competition for political and commercial control of Iran, and the two nations shored up a succession of weak and largely unpopular Qajar monarchs in return for a series of political, military, and commercial concessions.

These concessions and other aspects of Qajar rule angered the Iranian populace. The poor were burdened with heavy taxes that mainly served to support the court, not to strengthen Iran against foreign incursion or to build up an infrastructure. Iranian bazaar merchants and tradesmen (*bazaaris*) saw their livelihoods threatened by trade concessions and monopolies granted to Russia and Britian. The Shi'a clergy (*ulama*) were also dissatisfied, criticizing Qajar shahs for giving preference to foreign interests as well as for their decadent lifestyles and attempts to erode clerical power. The clergy were closely aligned with the *bazaaris* and served as natural leaders of the Shi'a population, whose loyalty to Islam tended to take precedence over loyalty to the Qajar state. Iranian intellectuals acquainted with the West also took issue with the Qajar government and began to call for European-style democratic, economic, and social reforms.

In 1891, general discontent with Qajar policy culminated in the Tobacco Protests, which broke out after Naser ad-Din Shah granted a British company full control over Iran's tobacco industry. The shah was forced to retract the concession when Iranians from all walks of life complied with a decree (*fatwa*) by the leading Shi'a cleric of the time that tobacco be boycotted. The widespread participation of general society, the leadership of the clergy, and the influence of *bazaaris* and westernizing reformers in these protests mirror many of the factors at play in the Iranian Revolution of 1979.

THE CONSTITUTIONAL REVOLUTION AND THE DISCOVERY OF OIL

The discontent that fostered the Tobacco Protests eventually led to the Constitutional Revolution of 1906. This revolution was the first of its kind in the Middle East, and it took place during the reign of Mozaffar ad-Din Shah, who ascended to the throne in 1896. Reforms enacted by the shah's ministers angered *bazaari*s, who felt that foreign trade was prioritized over Iranian trade. In late 1905 the discontent came to a rolling boil after the government decreed that two Tehran merchants be beaten for raising the price of sugar. The *bazaari*s went on strike, and in the following months the dissidents organized themselves and issued a series of demands, first for the establishment of a House of Justice to address the grievances of the population against the monarchy, and later for a full-fledged parliament and constitution. The shah buckled under popular pressure, and the first parliament opened in October 1906.

A merchant converses with friends outside his shop in Imam Khomeini square, Esfahan.

A constitution, based on the Belgian constitution, was signed into law shortly after.

The constitutional period was plagued by a lack of unity and clarity among those who desired reform. Secularist dissidents desired a western-style constitutional monarchy, but the reformist clergy supported less drastic reforms rooted in Islamic tradition. The constitution itself was deemed un-Islamic by prominent clergy who had initially supported reforms.

Foreign influence further complicated the constitutional period. At the turn of the twentieth century an Englishman of some wealth, William Knox D'Arcy, had been granted a concession by the shah for oil exploration in Iran. Oil was discovered in 1908. The Anglo-Persian Oil Company (which was later called the Anglo-Iranian Oil Company and is now known as British Petroleum) was formed the following year and went on to control Iran's petroleum resources for the next half century. Within a year of the establishment of Iran's first parliament, Britain and Russia signed a treaty dividing Iran in three spheres of influence: Russian in the northern and central regions, British in the southeast, and a neutral zone between. Iran was not consulted in the drawing up of the treaty.

From 1907 to 1911 a series of power struggles took place between parliament and various dissident groups on one hand, and Muhammad Ali Shah, who succeeded Mozaffar ad-Din, on the other. In December 1911, Russia, fearing that its interests were being compromised, dispatched troops toward Tehran, and the second parliament was dissolved. The constitutional period ended bleakly, but the changes it brought were to influence Iran for years to come.

REZA SHAH PAHLAVI

The years following the constitutional period brought increasing chaos in Iran. During WWI Iran declared its neutrality but quickly became a battlefield between Ottoman Turkey, Germany, Russia, and Britain. In 1915 Britain and Russia signed another secret treaty dividing control of Iran between themselves, and throughout the war the people of Iran suffered great deprivation and famine, partially as a result of occupation by foreign troops. In 1917, however, the Bolshevik Revolution led to Russia's withdrawal from treaties related to Iran, and the British moved to take complete control.

In 1921 the suffering of Iran's poor, the feebleness of its government, general hostility toward foreign incursions, and the desire for a strong central government created prime conditions for a coup d'etat. In February of that year, the journalist Sayyed Zia ad-Din Tabataba'i took over the Iranian government with the support of the Iranian Cossack Brigade, led by Reza Khan. Reza Khan rose quickly through the ranks of government, and in 1923 the shah reluctantly made him prime minister and then traveled to Europe in a move that amounted to abdication. In 1925, parliament formally ended the Qajar dynasty and proclaimed Reza Khan the first shah of the Pahlavi dynasty.

From 1925 to 1941 Reza Shah ruled as a dictator. Opposition or criticism of his rule was often rewarded by jail time or execution, and censorship was heavy handed. The new shah endeavored to strengthen and modernize Iran by making sweeping changes in nearly every facet of society. Some of his reforms met with success, especially in the transportation, communication, military, and industrial sectors, and his rise to power marked the first time an Iranian ruler possessed sufficient strength to ward off external threats to Iranian sovereignty. Reza Shah adopted a policy of playing British and Russian interests against one another, and he overturned a number of the concessions and treaties that had been signed to the detriment of Iran. Britain, however, retained control of Iran's southern oil reserves. Reza Shah also avoided foreign debt, but did so

Veiling in Iran: Prohibited and Compulsory *Hijab*

Since the revolution, Iranian law has required inhabitants of the country to observe Islamic standards of dress known as *hijab*. For women this means that everything but the face and hands should be covered while in public. Many in the West have heard stories of the harsh enforcement of Iran's veiling laws that occurred in the aftermath of the revolution as well as the less stringent crackdowns that have taken place in some urban areas in recent years. What many do not know is that a half century before the revolution, Iran's cities were the scene of dress code enforcement of a different kind.

In the 1930s, Reza Shah embarked on a tremendous effort to modernize Iran. His vision for a westernized Iran included his subjects exchanging their traditional dress for western clothing, and in 1936 he took the unprecedented step of ordering Iranian women to unveil. While some in Iran's educated urban classes embraced the change, the majority of Iran's population was outraged at the shah's trespass into his subjects' personal affairs. Gender segregation and the veiling of women had been the cultural norm in Iran for hundreds of years, and many women chose to stay in their homes rather than go out unveiled. Those who did venture out in their traditional clothing risked having their veils torn off by the shah's gendarmes. Reza Shah's policies had some liberating effects on middle- and upper-class women in Iran, but they served to alienate masses of ordinary Iranians and in some cases hindered the education of women, as many religious families opted to keep their daughters home rather than send them to school unveiled.

(continued on next page)

Muhammad Shah Pahlavi did not continue his father's policies of forced de-veiling, though he discouraged Islamic dress and supported equal rights for women as part of an overall push toward westernization. As the Pahlavi period progressed, greater numbers of educated women in Iran's cities and towns adopted western clothing, but veiling remained the norm for the majority of Iranian women. In the 1960s and 70s however, as discontent with Pahlavi rule increased, many women who had not previously veiled chose to do so out of a renewed interest in following Islamic principles or as a statement of protest against the regime. During the revolution, women turned out en masse to participate in demonstrations, and soon the chador, a distinctive tent-like veil usually made of black cloth, became a revolutionary symbol of resistance to tyranny.

In today's Iran veiling is a complex issue, and different manners of veiling can carry various political, cultural, and social overtones in addition to religious significance. Veiling-related tension tends to be concentrated in middle- and upper-class areas in Iran's larger cities, and many women in these populations strongly disagree with being forced by law to adhere to a clothing standard they find both restrictive and oppressive. Many other Iranian women of all educational and economic levels consciously embrace the veil, citing religious teachings and expressing their belief that covering allows them to be appreciated as people rather than objects. For many other women the veil is not a major concern but simply an accepted norm of their culture and religion.

primarily by increasing the tax burden shouldered by Iran's poorest, who benefited little from his reign. The shah himself acquired vast wealth.

Reza Shah's educational, social, judicial, and bureaucratic changes were embraced by many in the wealthier urban classes but tended to contradict the values of average Iranians and rouse the ire of the clergy. The shah sought to marginalize the clergy's leadership and distance Iranian society from the Shi'a Islamic elements of its identity. In doing so, however, he alienated the large portion of society for whom Shi'a Islam was central. The ideological and economic divides between the westernized, wealthy elite and the masses of Iran's conservative poor was something that would plague Iranian society for decades and contribute to the conditions creating the 1979 revolution.

In the years leading up to WWII, Reza Shah increasingly oriented himself toward Germany, and by 1940 that country was heavily involved in trade and industry within Iran. This greatly disturbed Britain and the Soviet Union, which demanded that Germans be expelled from Iran. When Reza Shah refused, the two countries' armies invaded, and Reza Shah was forced to abdicate in favor of his son, Muhammad Shah Pahlavi.

THE 1953 COUP

For the remainder of WWII, the allies largely controlled Iran. Foreign troops taxed the country's resources, and famine became a reality for many Iranians. When WWII ended, Britain, Russia, and the United States turned their focus on the country's oil resources.

In the first years of his reign, Muhammad Shah Pahlavi proved less a dictator than his father, and as WWII ended, parliament and press experienced greater freedom. Iranians used this freedom to criticize foreign control of oil resources, in particular the stranglehold of the Anglo-Iranian Oil Company

(AIOC) over Iranian oil. This issue came to a head in the early 1950s, when the National Front coalition, running on a platform of nationalizing the country's oil resources and strengthening democracy in Iran, won a large number of seats in parliament. A short time later parliament voted to nationalize the country's oil resources and dissolve the agreement with AIOC. Less than a month after the vote, the coalition's intensely popular leader, Muhammad Mossadeq, became prime minister.

The AIOC and British government were strongly opposed to oil nationalization and began immediate attempts to depose Mossadeq. Britain led a boycott of Iranian oil that it backed with gunboats in the Persian Gulf. Despite a ruling by the International Court of Justice in Iran's favor, the United States sided with Britain in the dispute. Attempts to reach a settlement between the AIOC and the Iranian government failed, and the Iranian government severed diplomatic ties with Britain in 1952.

The oil crisis worsened Iran's already severe economic problems, and the Mossadeq government, weakened by opposition from the British and shah, failed to make many needed economic and social reforms. Mossadeq sought to shore up his power by requesting emergency powers and control over the ministry of war, resigning when his requests were denied. He was soon reinstated, however, following nationwide demonstrations in his support.

In early 1953, the Central Intelligence Agency (CIA) at the behest of British intelligence sources, planned a coup to overthrow Mossadeq. In an operation code-named Ajax, the CIA, with British support, carried out a propaganda war in Iran against Mossadeq and persuaded the shah to dismiss the prime minister. The plan backfired, and the shah fled the country. Britain, the CIA, and their Iranian allies stepped up their efforts, and on August 19, 1953, a CIA-supported crowd, joined by anti-Mossadeq elements in the Iranian army as well as other Iranians

Iran and WWII: A Novel

Savushun was published in 1969 and has been a best-selling book in Iran ever since. Written by female author Simin Daneshvar, the novel tells the story of Zari, a woman whose life in the city of Shiraz revolves around family relationships, domestic duties, and charity work in a mental hospital.

As the book progresses, the harsh realities of life in WWII-era Iran impact the lives of Zari and her family more and more dramatically. Iran's people face famine and hardship, and Allied powers pressure the country's landowners to surrender valuable resources to feed and sustain occupying troops. Yosuf, Zari's headstrong and principled husband, refuses to sell food needed by his tenants to the British, and his unwillingness to compromise his principles ends in tragedy.

Two translations of *Savushun* have been published in English (see *A Persian Requiem* in the Resources section), and each gives readers a valuable glimpse into Iranian society, culture, and history. The novel examines western impact on Iran as well as the influence of capitalism and communism on an Islamic society, but it is foremost a story of a woman finding the inner strength and courage to stand on principle in the face of adversity.

opposed to Mossadeq, attacked various government buildings, offices, and Mossadeq's home. The prime minister surrendered the following day, and the shah was firmly reinstated. This marked the beginning of large-scale involvement by the United States as well as a turning point in Iranian sentiment toward the United States. Until this time the United States had been viewed by many Iranians as a positive "third force" in their struggle to shake off Russian and British economic and political intervention. After Operation Ajax, however, the United States began to be seen as one of a line of western countries determined to pursue its own agenda at the expense of the interests of the Iranian people.

MUHAMMAD SHAH PAHLAVI

Following the 1953 coup, the United States became the leading foreign power involved in Iran. An oil deal was brokered between Iran and a consortium of foreign oil companies (mostly British and American) in which profits were shared fifty-fifty between the consortium and Iran. At the same time, Muhammad Shah became increasingly dictatorial and established an intelligence service known as SAVAK in 1957. In subsequent decades SAVAK was responsible for the torture, imprisonment, and execution of thousands of dissidents from across the political and religious spectrum.

In 1963, Muhammad Shah embarked on a series of land, industrial, and social reforms known as the White Revolution. Many Iranians adamantly opposed the reforms on the grounds that they violated Iranian cultural norms and Islamic principles. Opposition was led by clerics, in particular the influential Ayatollah Ruhollah Khomeini. On June 5, 1963, Khomeini delivered a famous speech in condemnation of the shah. The cleric was arrested two days later, and his detention sparked large-scale riots in which hundreds of demonstrators were killed by the shah's troops. Khomeini was released after eight months only to be arrested again in November 1964 after vociferously criticizing an agreement between Iran and the United States that would make U.S. military personnel in the country immune from Iranian law. This time, he was forced into exile and remained outside Iran until his return in 1979.

Having suppressed all significant protest, the shah went forward with his reforms, which brought positive changes in education and women's rights as well as in infrastructure and business. The 1960s and 70s was a time of tremendous oil revenues and economic growth for Iran, but corruption in the royal family and government circles was rampant, and the gap between Iran's rich and poor grew wider. The shah prioritized large, ostentatious development projects to the detriment of more practical, smaller-scale alternatives. Many reforms were based on western models, particularly in the area of agriculture, and were highly unsuited to the Iranian landscape. In addition, vast amounts of oil revenue were funneled into a bloated military budget. The rural and tribal poor migrated en masse to Iran's urban centers, which were plagued by tremendous housing and energy shortages. Many of the poor also continued to go without basic healthcare and education, and unemployment and inflation levels were very high. Iranians criticized United States' business involvement in Iran as well as the shah's dependence on that country. Foreigners came to Iran in growing numbers to fill jobs in business and government-related sectors and were targets of resentment, both because they were given privileged access to housing and other commodities out of the reach of ordinary Iranians, and also because they engaged in behaviors that violated social and religious norms. By the late 1970s, popular discontent rooted in these realities culminated in an outbreak of opposition to the shah and calls for wide-reaching reform.

II. The Islamic Revolution

FACTIONS

The Iranian Revolution was a movement involving many different individuals and groups with varying goals and ideologies. These groups cooperated during the late 1970s with the common aims of reforming the government and ousting the shah. Once these goals were achieved and the new government began to take shape, however, differing ideologies became sources of conflict.

The face that quickly came to symbolize the revolution, both in Iran and abroad, was that of Ayatollah Ruhollah Khomeini, who struck a deep chord with his fellow Iranians and achieved

A coppersmith plies his trade in Esfahan's Grand Bazaar.

A spice seller in his shop in Esfahan's Grand Bazaar. Iranian cuisine utilizes a wide array of herbs and spices, and the country is renowned for the high-quality saffron it produces.

mass support in a way unmatched by any other group or individual. Khomeini's intense popularity helped to secure the **clergy's** leading role in the revolution.

The ideas and actions of lay Iranian individuals and groups were also an integral part of the revolutionary movement. Iranian **intellectuals** had for years decried Pahlavi corruption, autocracy, and dependence on the West. Shi'a identity was paramount for many prominent intellectuals, who creatively reinterpreted Islamic principles to answer the political and social challenges of Iranian society. Other thinkers were more secular in orientation. Most intellectuals espoused democratic, constitutionalist, and nationalistic ideals, and many were influenced heavily by leftist ideologies.

Guerrilla groups, most notably the Mujahedin-e Khalq and the Fedaiyan-e Khalq, also took part in the revolution. These groups, whose ideologies were rooted in Marxism and/or radical interpretations of Islam, had emerged in the wake of the harsh government crackdowns of 1963. Their members supported violent action to overthrow the Pahlavi government.

Iranian **students**, both at home and abroad, were key players in dissident movements, and they were inspired by anti-shah intellectuals, the clergy (particularly Khomeini), and, in some cases, the guerilla groups.

Bazaaris, who tended to hold traditional values and align themselves with the clergy, put considerable resources and influence at the disposal of the opposition.

As the revolution picked up speed, the masses of Iran's poor and disenfranchised rallied behind Khomeini. These average Iranians, who turned out in the millions to demonstrate against the shah in 1978, viewed their struggle through the lens of Shi'a history and expressed their opposition in the explicitly religious terminology of Khomeini.

EVENTS

In 1977 general discontent began to show itself in more open ways, with letters and petitions denouncing the Pahlavi government and its human rights violations in wide circulation. The revolution was sparked in earnest in January 1978 when an article appeared in a government newspaper accusing Khomeini of crimes against the state. Public outcry against the article was immediate, and seminary students in Qom demonstrated in protest. Demonstrators were confronted with violence, and some were killed by police. The deaths of these students began a cycle of demonstrations that took place in forty-day intervals, based on Shi'a mourning customs. Protestors often destroyed government property but were generally nonviolent toward human beings. Security forces, on the other hand, killed thousands of protestors over the course of the year.

Early on September 8, 1978, Muhammad Shah declared martial law and forbade all demonstrations. That same day a massive protest occurred in Tehran, and government forces opened fire on thousands of demonstrators in Jaleh Square. After Black Friday, as the event is now known, protest became even more widespread, involving millions of people from all regions of the country. The shah vacillated between suppressing opposition and making concessions to protestors' demands, but the tide had turned in favor of the revolution. Khomeini's voice from exile in Najaf became increasingly influential, and the shah pressured Iraqi authorities to deport him. In early October Khomeini traveled to France, where he received wide media attention.

On December 2, millions gathered in Tehran to demand the departure of the shah and the return of Khomeini. On January 16, 1979, knowing his regime was doomed, the shah left Iran. Scarcely two weeks later, after fifteen years of exile, Khomeini returned to his homeland.

Remembering the Iranian Revolution

Haydeh Javandel, above, is a native of northwestern Iran who now resides in Qom. Here she shares her experiences as one of many young women across Iran who supported the revolution.

In the time leading up to the Islamic Revolution, I had become acquainted with some Muslim activists at the Technological University of Urumiyeh. These activists were providing instruction in Islamic teachings and giving women headscarves and coats, as they were not available at that time in the shops. When I decided to start veiling, I received a secondhand coat from my friend, which I in turn gave to another girl. At that time, those who wore Islamic covering were considered strange, and other girls would even ridicule them. We participated in protest demonstrations in Urumiyeh, and in one of them my brother was stabbed by an anti-revolutionary and had to be sent to the hospital. It was a very scary period, and no one knew what was going to happen. I remember feeling that we were living in a time when the 2,500-year history of the shahs was coming to an end. It is one thing to read about such things in books, but another to experience it in one's life.

(continued on next page)

In those days we thought the most difficult thing would be to make a revolution. Later, however, we realized that maintaining the ideals of the revolution was even more difficult, especially after we were attacked by Iraq, and especially when we saw that Saddam was supported by so many different countries that gave Iraq planes, chemical weapons, and other instruments of war. My little brother was injured by chemical weapons during the war, as were many, many other Iranian soldiers and villagers. Today we are still struggling to maintain our freedom and independence.

The Formation of an Islamic Republic

For the masses of Iranians who opposed the shah, Khomeini's return was the emotional climax of the revolution. An atmosphere of euphoria prevailed among the millions of supporters who congregated to meet the ayatollah at the Tehran airport. Khomeini was recognized as the leader of the revolution, and as such he was confronted by the complex political realities of a country in transition between two governments. On February 4, Khomeini announced the formation of an interim government (the "Provisional Revolutionary Government") headed by moderate Mehdi Bazargan. Fighting broke out between pro-shah and pro-Khomeini factions in the military, and the latter were aided by various revolutionary groups, including the Mujahedin-e Khalq and Fedaiyan-e Khalq. On February 11 (now considered the anniversary of the revolution) top military commanders declared the armed forces' neutrality in political matters, and the remnants of the shah's government disintegrated. Over the next several years, as elements in the new regime sought to enforce traditional Islamic values and purge the country of western influences, hundreds of thousands of middle- and upper-class Iranian families who did not embrace this vision emigrated to the West.

At the end of March 1979, the Bazargan government, under Khomeini's direction, held a national referendum in which the Iranian people voted for or against the formation of an Islamic republic. The results were overwhelmingly in favor of an Islamic republic, though the exact nature of such a republic was still in question. Meanwhile, differences between the moderate interim government and those who shared Khomeini's more radical views began to show. Bazargan and other moderates expressed concern over the summary trials and executions of counter-revolutionaries at the hands of the newly formed judiciary. Of further concern to the interim government were the actions of the *komiteh*s (see sidebar on pages 43-44).

The framing of a new constitution was also an area of dispute. An early draft of the constitution was essentially a non-monarchal version of the 1906-07 document, but the final draft presented to the people by an Assembly of Experts elected in summer 1979 was substantially different. The newly formed constitution enshrined the concept of *velayat-e faqih* (see sidebar) and gave a great deal of governmental authority to a top cleric known as the supreme leader. Liberal and secular forces stridently opposed the constitution and the concept of *velayat-e faqih*, as did some senior Shi'a clergy. Masses of ordinary Iranians, however, continued to support Khomeini and the constitution that had his approval. In addition, many people were angered by the interim government's lack of focus on the poor and needed social reforms, as well as its willingness to improve relations with the United States.

Iranian-U.S. relations became a point of heated contention when President Carter allowed the ex-shah to enter the United States for cancer treatment, and anger against the United States crystallized on November 4, 1979, when a group of radical students occupied the United States' embassy in Tehran and took its personnel hostage (see chapter 4 for more detailed information on the hostage crisis). Bazargan and his cabinet resigned in protest over the hostage affair, which, along with the 1980 invasion of Iran by Iraq, galvanized the country behind Khomeini. In December 1979 the constitution was put to popular vote and officially adopted as the law of the land. Demonstrations in protest, in particular a series of large uprisings in Tabriz, were suppressed.

Over the next several years, the political course of Iran was rocky. Rumors of coup plots were rife in the spring and summer of 1980, and one was uncovered in June, followed by another in July. Then, in September, Iraq invaded Iran. The Iranian government rallied in defense despite substantial internal political

Twelver Shi'a Muslims and Politics: The Rule of the Jurist

Velayat-e faqih (commonly translated as the "rule of the jurist") is a term that refers to a Shi'a doctrine of Islamic government developed by Ayatollah Khomeini in the late 1960s. This doctrine states that Muslim jurists (high-ranking clerics) should provide political as well as spiritual leadership to Muslim communities. In particular, Khomeini believed that a single, most qualified jurist should oversee the political affairs of Islamic society. The present-day Iranian government, in which the office of supreme leader (held first by Khomeini and now by Ayatollah Ali Khamanei) is the most powerful in the land, is organized on the principles of *velayat-e faqih*.

Khomeini rooted his conception of *velayat-e faqih* in Shi'a beliefs about the authority of the twelve imams (see chapter 1, page 18). Shi'a Muslims believe that after the death of Prophet Muhammad the imams were divinely appointed to carry on the leadership (*velayat*) of the Muslim community. Many Shi'a believe that this leadership was meant to be political as well as spiritual. But the imams for the most part lived (and were often imprisoned under) Sunni rule, and their followers, as a minority community in the midst of a sometimes hostile majority, tended toward political quietism. When the final imam, known as the Mahdi, went into hiding in the ninth century, the question arose as to who would lead the Shi'a community. It is widely believed that this responsibility was passed on to the clergy, in particular to senior clerics known as "sources of emulation,"

(continued on next page)

41

who provide spiritual guidance and Islamic legal guidance to lay Shi'a.

Following the disappearance of the twelfth imam, the Shi'a clergy exercised wide-ranging leadership over their communities, though those communities were still subject to non-Shi'a governmental authority. The advent of the Safavid dynasty at the turn of the sixteenth century and the subsequent transformation of Iran into a uniquely Shi'a country brought additional power to the Shi'a clergy, and they became a force with which the Safavid, Qajar, and Pahlavi monarchs had to reckon. However, it wasn't until Khomeini that a strong case was made that the clergy should have direct political rule.

When the revolution in Iran began, what shape the new government would take was not clear. Though Khomeini was intent on implementing *velayat-e faqih*, he also seemed concerned with incorporating democratic elements into the Iranian government. The constitution reflects this tension, supporting both theocratic and democratic elements in the governmental structures of Iran. The bulk of political power, however, is in the hands of the supreme leader, considered by proponents of *velayat-e faqih* to be the instrument of the divine in human political affairs.

Since the time of the revolution, *velayat-e faqih* has been articulated in a variety of ways, with some thinkers emphasizing a democratic process of electing a *faqih*. Other Shi'a scholars and clerics reject the doctrine out of hand, believing instead that the clergy should play an advisory role in the government or abstain from direct political involvement altogether.

conflict and an armed forces in a post-revolutionary state of disarray.

Abolhassan Bani Sadr, a non-cleric and close associate of Khomeini during the latter's time in France, was elected to the presidency by a substantial margin in January 1980, but he and his supporters were quickly locked in a power struggle with the powerful Islamic Republican Party (IRP) under the leadership of Chief Supreme Court Justice Ayatollah Muhammad Beheshti. Khomeini, who was ideologically more aligned with the IRP, urged the two sides to compromise for the sake of unity, particularly following the invasion by Iraq. Such compromise proved short-lived, and Bani Sadr became increasingly vociferous in his denunciation of clerical rule. By late spring of 1981, he challenged the rule of Khomeini himself, and parliament moved to impeach the president.

Bani Sadr's supporters and others opposed to the government, including the MEK, called on Iranians to demonstrate on June 20, 1981, the day of parliament impeachment vote. During the demonstrations, fighting broke out between the guerillas and the Revolutionary Guard. About twenty demonstrators were killed and many more were arrested. Bani Sadr was impeached and went into hiding. One week later IRP headquarters was bombed by dissidents, and more than seventy people, including Ayatollah Beheshti, were killed.

These events set into motion a conflict between the government and leftist guerilla groups that ended in the deaths of thousands of people. Guerilla groups assassinated government officials and religious leaders, including the popular Mohammad Ali Raja'i, who had succeeded Bani Sadr as president. The larger public reacted angrily to the tactics of the guerillas, and the government went on a country-wide crackdown against the leftists, executing thousands in the subsequent months. Eventually the uprising was put down, and by the end of 1982 most serious internal opposition to the government had been quelled, leaving Khomeini and his supporters firmly in control.

III. The Structure of the Iranian Government

The structure of the Iranian government contains democratic as well as authoritarian components. A supreme leader has power over every aspect of government, but he is accountable, in theory at least, to a popularly elected Assembly of Experts that could depose him should he fail to meet certain criteria outlined in the constitution. The president and parliament are even more democratically accountable, and several times since the revolution the voting process has significantly altered the face of the Iranian government.

The government is complex, and it has many centers of power. The constitution adopted in 1979 and revised in 1989 outlines the organization and delineates the powers and limits of each of the various branches of the government.

The most powerful office of the government is that of the **supreme leader,** to whom the constitution gives the responsibility for the general oversight of all governmental affairs. The supreme leader appoints the head of the judiciary as well as the heads of state-controlled media and half the members of the important Guardian Council. He also acts as commander-in-chief of the military, police, and security forces and is the only figure permitted by the constitution to declare war. The supreme leader also possesses broad veto powers and the ability to intervene in matters related to parliament and other branches of government. In practice however, both Khomeini, the first supreme leader, and Ali Khamane'i, his successor, have opted against involving themselves directly in the day-to-day affairs of the government, preferring to intervene only in select cases deemed to be of particular importance. The supreme leader is elected and advised

The *Komiteh*s and the Cultural Revolution

Immediately following the revolution, Khomeini and many of the revolutionaries turned their focus from ousting the shah to purging Iranian society from influences that were seen as non-Islamic. This movement was known as the Cultural Revolution, and a large number of loosely associated groups known as "*komiteh*s" (committees) were influential in this effort. The *komiteh*s were grassroots organizations that sprung up in the late 1970s from mosques, schools, and workplaces with the goals of supporting the revolution, protecting protestors from government toughs, and distributing aid to the needy.

At the end of the revolution, some *komiteh* members armed themselves with weapons procured during the brief period of fighting between pro-shah military forces and revolutionaries and went on to arrest a large number of officials and others linked to the monarchy. The Bazargan government opposed vigilante actions by the *komiteh*s, and in late February 1979, Khomeini stated that the groups should curtail their actions once the new government was in firm control. In the summer of 1979, however, he opted instead to centralize and purge the *komiteh*s of elements opposed to his ideology, and over the next several years the *komiteh*s continued to act against those who opposed the regime, including leftist groups and Kurds and Turks who demanded greater autonomy. The activities of the *komiteh*s were further centralized in 1984, when their focus changed to enforcing morality and social laws

(continued on next page)

(specifically the veiling of women) and combating smuggling and drug trafficking. In 1991 the *komitehs* were absorbed into Iran's regular law enforcement bodies.

Efforts to purge Iranian society from non-Islamic influences focused particularly on the country's universities, which had been centers of leftist thought and activity. In 1980, Khomeini issued an ultimatum to leftist sympathizers on university campuses, and following his speech vigilante groups violently took over some campuses, forcing out leftist groups and faculty members with the result that some were injured or killed.

Subsequently, Khomeini formed a body known as the Council of the Cultural Revolution, which shut down the universities for several years, reopening them after faculty who disagreed with revolutionary ideologies had been purged and books deemed subversive had been banned. Under the new system students and staff were required to adhere to an Islamic lifestyle and demonstrate loyalty to the Islamic government. Non-Muslims were required to refrain from violating Islamic norms and were banned from many fields of study. The Cultural Revolution also greatly affected the media, which was Islamized and brought under government control.

The Cultural Revolution sparked many of the intelligentsia to leave the country, and its legacy continues to affect higher education in Iran. The government's control of the universities decreased somewhat in the 1990s and the first few years of the new millennium, but the last several years has seen greater restrictions imposed upon the academic community.

by an eighty-six member body of senior clerics known as the **Assembly of Experts,** which has the power to depose the supreme leader should he fail to meet any of the qualifications of office as outlined in the constitution. Members of the Assembly of Experts are popularly elected to eight-year terms of office.

The **executive branch** is the most powerful office in Iran after that of the supreme leader. Iran's presidents are popularly elected and must achieve a simple majority of the vote. The president has the power to appoint and dismiss a wide variety of officials including the heads of Iran's various government ministries as well as ten vice presidents who head up a variety of political organizations related to cultural, governmental, social, and other affairs. Presidential appointments are subject to approval by parliament, and in turn, the presidential signature is required in order for the bills passed by parliament to be executed.

The **legislative branch** of the government is composed of the popularly elected parliament, which is responsible for drafting and passing laws, ratifying international treaties, and approving the government's budget.

The **judiciary** is comprised of several different kinds of courts in which judges, who must meet Islamic legal qualifications, decide the case in question in accordance with applicable laws. According to the constitution, the laws of Iran are based on and must not contradict Ja'fari Shi'a Islamic law (which itself is subject to a wide range of interpretations), but a substantial portion of the laws are related to the day-to-day affairs of running a modern nation-state and thus are outside the scope of traditional Islamic jurisprudence.

The **Guardian Council** is a powerful player in Iranian politics, and its role and actions are the subject of much debate and criticism both inside and outside Iran. Composed of six clerics appointed by the supreme leader and six legal experts elected by parliament, the Guardian Council has the responsibility of accepting or vetoing all bills passed by parliament. Laws are evaluated based on conformity to Islamic law and the Iranian constitution. In addition, the power to interpret the constitution lies in the hands of the Guardian Council. The Guardian Council is also responsible for vetting candidates for the presidency, parliament, and the Assembly of Experts. Many accuse the Guardian Council of disqualifying reformist and liberal candidates based on questionable criteria and thus predisposing election results in favor of conservatives. Others point out that in a country like Iran, where party affiliation and personal wealth are less a factor in bringing candidates to the forefront of a race, practicality necessitates that the government narrow the field of candidates from hundreds or thousands to a manageable number of qualified candidates. Critics of the Guardian Council feel that it wields too much power, and that its power is heavily weighted in favor of clerical conservatives.

In 1988 an **Expediency Council** was formed to end legislative stalemates between parliament and the Guardian Council. The members of the Expediency Council are appointed by the supreme leader, and in addition to playing a mediating role between parliament and Guardian Council, they serve as an advisory body to the supreme leader and, as of 2005, have some supervisory powers over all branches of government.

IV. Ayatollah Ruhollah Khomeini

For millions of Iranians, Ayatollah Ruhollah Khomeini was not merely a political leader but a beloved and deeply spiritual man whose struggle to bring justice to the oppressed and fulfill religious ideals was (and remains) a source of great inspiration. Khomeini's charisma was evident long before the revolution when, as a young teacher in the Shi'a seminary, he was surrounded by devoted followers. In the years leading up to the

A black turban signifies that this Shi'a cleric is a descendant of Prophet Muhammad.

Some of the personal effects of Ayatollah Khomeini, on display in his Tehran home.

revolution, more and more people from all walks of life were attracted to this outspoken cleric who gave voice to their frustrations and longings, and by the time Khomeini returned from exile to Iran in 1979, he was ecstatically hailed as leader by millions who saw the potential that their dreams of justice and well-being would be fulfilled. The decade following the revolution was a troubled one for Iran, but masses of Iranians continued to love and support Khomeini, as was evidenced by the staggering display of collective grief by the millions that flocked to attend his funeral.

This portrait of a charismatic, justice-seeking Khomeini could not be more different than the impressions most westerners have of the leader of the Iranian Revolution. North Americans and Europeans who witnessed the revolution from outside Iran saw a stern-faced, fanatical Khomeini who imposed a harsh version of Islamic law on his people, called the United States the "Great Satan" and presided over large crowds chanting "Death to America."

The great variety of views of Khomeini bears witness to the complexity of this important figure. He was born to a well-established clerical family in the small Iranian town of Khomein in 1902. Khomeini's father was murdered before Ruhollah was a year old, and in 1918 Khomeini's mother and aunt, both strong women who played prominent roles in his life, died in a cholera epidemic. Following family tradition, Khomeini enrolled in the Shi'a seminary system at the age of seventeen, studying first in the city of Arak, and later in Qom, a prominent center of Shi'a scholarship. Khomeini showed a great aptitude for Greek and Islamic philosophy in addition to traditional religious topics, and an avid interest in Persian poetry and Islamic mysticism helped shape his spiritual life and thought. In 1929 he married Batoul Saqafi, and the couple had seven children, five of whom survived infancy.

By his early thirties, Khomeini had achieved the status of *mujtahid*, or qualified interpreter of Islamic law. He remained in Qom where he taught and rose to prominence in clerical circles. As Khomeini witnessed the secularizing policies of Reza Shah, the 1953 coup of the Mossadeq government, and the increasingly dictatorial and westernizing rule of Muhammad Shah Pahlavi, he grew more and more critical of the political state of affairs in Iran. In 1962, following the death of the most senior Shi'a cleric, Grand Ayatollah Borujerdi, Khomeini emerged as a senior religious leader, and by 1963 he was outspoken in his opposition to the Pahlavi government. His arrest and subsequent exile only increased his popularity, and he continued to be a voice of opposition from exile in Turkey, Iraq, and France.

Khomeini's political and religious views evolved over time and were influenced by many factors. His revolutionary vision was made up of complex spiritual, political, and material goals. He sought to deliver the poor from their poverty but maintained that the primary goal of the revolution was not economic prosperity. He waged jihad against those whom he considered enemies of Islam but argued that internal jihad against one's base desires is far more important. Khomeini authored the concept of *velayat-e faqih* (see sidebar on pages 41-42), but espoused democratic ideals and at times pushed for less clerical involvement in the post-revolutionary government. He utilized harsh rhetoric against his enemies but encouraged compromise where he believed it was possible.

Khomeini lived an extremely simple life, and his rejection of wealth and the material trappings of political leadership contrasts sharply with the lifestyle of the shah that preceded him. His supporters point to the largely peaceful nature of the revolution leading up to the departure of the shah, and argue that harsh measures afterward were necessitated from the standpoint of national security. Detractors point to the thousands of members

Pilgrims in the courtyard of the shrine of Lady Fatima Ma'sumeh in Qom.

of the opposition who were executed with Khomeini's tacit approval and argue that he needlessly prolonged the Iran-Iraq war, resulting in much unnecessary death and deprivation. Some Iranians, including many in the large exile community in the West, remain deeply critical of Khomeini, but many others, including prominent reformers, find inspiration in various parts of his legacy. Any well-rounded view of Khomeini must take into account not only the complexity of the ayatollah's life and thought but also the complexity and challenges of the era in which he lived and ruled.

A banner displayed during Muharram, the month in which Shi'a Muslims mourn the death of Imam Hussein, grandson of Prophet Muhammad. This banner depicts the Iranian flag at the top, under which is a portrait of Ayatollahs Khomeini and Khamane'i. Beneath this is a scene from the battle of Karbela, in which Hussein was killed, and the field of tulips at bottom serves as a symbol of martyrs.

An Iranian family strolls through Esfahan's Grand Bazaar.

Iran Since the Revolution

In Esfahan, a massive cemetery houses the remains of Iranian soldiers killed in the Iran-Iraq war. Grave markers bear portraits of the dead, many of whom were teenagers when they became casualties of this devastating conflict.

3. IRAN SINCE THE REVOLUTION

I. The Iran-Iraq War

The Iran-Iraq war, which began scarcely a year after the revolution, exacted a terrible toll on the Iranian people and played a crucial role in forming the character of the Islamic republic in the first decade of its existence.

Historians and analysts point to a variety of causes for the war, including centuries-old disputes over the Iran-Iraq border. The largest of these disputes was related to the important Shatt al-Arab, a waterway which provides the largely landlocked Iraq with vital access to the Persian Gulf and serves the port city of Khorramshahr, from which Iranian oil mined in the province of Khuzestan makes its way to the Gulf. Khuzestan itself had been disputed territory for several centuries, and water rights in other border regions were also a source of tension. A border treaty signed in 1975 had terms in Iran's favor and was a source of resentment for Iraq, particularly in light of the fact that Iran failed to return some of the territory allocated to Iraq under the conditions of that treaty. A series of border clashes took place in the summer of 1980, and the war began in earnest when Iraq launched a full-scale invasion of Iran on September 22, 1980.

A variety of factors other than territorial disputes also contributed to the war, including the diametrically opposed ideologies and values of Iranian and Iraqi leaders and governments. The Iraqi government was largely secular and nationalistic, whereas Iran was headed by a revolutionary establishment intent on ruling according to religious principles. The relationship between Saddam Hussein and Ayatollah Khomeini had long been strained. Saddam Hussein had, at the shah's bidding, forced Khomeini out of Iraq in 1978, and Khomeini repeatedly criticized the Ba'ath regime as tyrannical and irreligious. Both leaders and nations had a great deal of pride at stake in the war. In Iran, the conflict was considered a supreme test of the principles of the revolution, the chance to encourage Islamic revolutions across the Muslim world, and a sacred battle to defend nation and religion against aggression and blasphemy. Under Hussein's leadership, Iraq sought to promote Arab nationalism and become a superpower in the region, something a victory over Iran could conceivably accomplish. Furthermore, the Ba'ath regime viewed the invasion as a preemptive war of defense against Iranian attempts to export the Islamic revolution to Iraq. Hussein feared that the Shi'a Muslims making up 60 percent of Iraq's population might revolt against the Sunni-dominated Ba'ath government.

This complex set of disputes led to an eight-year war in which over a million Iranian and Iraqi soldiers and civilians were killed and many more wounded and injured. The economic costs were also staggering. Each country spent the equivalent of hundreds of billions of dollars on the war effort. Iraq went deeply into debt for the purchase of arms, and Iran's industrial infrastructure was greatly damaged by Iraqi bombs. To this day the country's oil production remains affected by the war.

The war was waged in a series of offensives and stalemates, and at its end neither country emerged as winner. The Iraqis initially held the upper hand, controlling fourteen thousand square kilometers of Iranian territory within a month of the invasion, including the city of Khorramshahr. Saddam Hussein had factored the post-revolutionary disarray of Iran's military into the timing of his attack and probably underestimated Iranian popular support for the revolutionary government. As it happened, Iranians rallied behind Khomeini and volunteered by the tens of thousands to repel the Iraqi forces. By June 1982 the Iraqi army had been driven from nearly all Iranian territory. Iran then pushed into Iraqi territory, aiming to capture the city of Basra and depose the Ba'ath regime. Iraqi defenses, however, proved difficult to penetrate, and the remainder of the land war was characterized by a series of long, bloody battles and offenses by both sides in which only small amounts of territory exchanged hands.

Iraq's military was much stronger than that of Iran, particularly in terms of equipment, and Iraqi weapons purchases were four times that of Iran during the course of the war. This was mainly because Iraq had a great deal of international support as well as free access to the world's arms market, while a series of arms embargos forced Iran to purchase inferior weaponry at higher prices on the black market. Iran's population, however, was much larger than that of Iraq and much more dedicated to the war effort.

Iran suffered immense casualties throughout the war as a result of human wave tactics in which thousands upon thousands of poorly equipped but highly dedicated volunteers rushed heavily fortified enemy positions. These volunteers, including young boys and old men, went into battle with the deep religious conviction that death would be martyrdom in the tradition of the followers of Hussein at Karbala.

As the war dragged on, the human and economic costs grew. In 1985, Saddam launched bombing raids on Iranian cities, to which Iran responded in kind, with the result that both sides suffered civilian casualties. Each side also attacked shipping in the Persian Gulf. Iraq was favored in the war by the American government, and this "tanker war," as it is known, prompted the involvement of the U.S. Navy in the conflict.

In July 1987 the United Nations Security Council passed U.S.-sponsored Resolution 598, which called for a cessation of hostilities and return to 1975 boundaries. Iraq, whose population's support for the war had long since waned, accepted the terms of the resolution, but Iran, which had recently experienced gains in the north, failed to respond. A short time later, Iraq renewed its bombings of Iranian cities and mounted several successful ground offenses. By this time, the morale of the Iranian people had undergone a series of severe blows. Civilians had suffered for years under extreme privation and war-related shortages, as well as bombing raids on major cities. Widespread Iraqi use of chemical weapons, in blatant violation of international law, also dealt a heavy blow to Iranian spirits, and the pool of volunteers, so strong in the war's early years, had declined. Voices inside Iran began increasingly to call for an end to the war.

On July 3, 1988, the USS *Vincennes*, deployed to the Gulf by the United States as part of the tanker war, shot down Iran Air Flight 655, killing all 290 people aboard, including sixty-six children. Shortly after, a demoralized Khomeini, who had long viewed waging the war as a religious duty and a vital component of the revolution, was finally induced to consider a diplomatic end to the war. On July 18, 1988, Iran announced its unconditional acceptance of U.N. Resolution 598, and peace was established on August 20, 1988.

The effect of the Iran-Iraq war on the Iranian people is hard to overestimate. Millions of Iranians lost family members and friends to the war, and the damage to the country's infrastructure and economy was immense. Tens of thousands of Iranians wounded on the battlefield have continued to suffer physically and psychologically to this day, with many still living with the gruesome consequences of exposure to chemical weapons. The war served to unify the Iranian public and galvanize them behind Khomeini, but the elderly ayatollah and many of his followers were devastated by its stalemated end.

II. Politics, Economics, and Society in Post-Revolutionary Iran

POLITICS

Politics in the Islamic Republic of Iran was characterized by turmoil in the years immediately following the revolution. By 1982, however, the government had been stabilized, with power transitions taking place in a more orderly fashion according to election schedules. Issues that have dominated the Iranian political scene in the decades since the revolution include the Iran-Iraq war, economic policy, relations with foreign powers, and social freedoms.

Presidents

Within two years of the revolution, the Islamic Republic's first three presidents had resigned (Bazargan), been impeached (Bani Sadr) or were assassinated (Raja'i). The October 1981 election of **Ali Khamanei**, a close associate of Khomeini and the first cleric to become president, ushered in a succession of long-term presidential administrations. Khamanei's two terms in office spanned nearly the entire length of the Iran-Iraq war. After the death of Khomeini in 1989, Khamanei stepped down from the presidency two months before the scheduled end of his term in order to assume the position of supreme leader.

Following the promotion of Khamanei to supreme leader, **Akbar Hashemi Rafsanjani** was elected president. Generally considered a social conservative who favored pragmatism on

Top: Two men play chess outside a mosque in Tabriz.

Bottom: One of Iran's many dry bread collectors arranges his cart. Islam discourages waste, and Iranian families give or sell uneaten pieces of bread to be used as animal feed.

issues related to the economy and foreign policy, Rafsanjani worked to privatize the state-controlled Iranian economy and improve relations between Iran and the outside world during his two terms as president. A prominent force in Iranian politics since the revolution, Rafsanjani has held a variety of other important offices. Recently his centrist views have pitted him against the current president, Mahmoud Ahmadinejad.

Muhammad Khatami, who was elected in 1997 and served two terms, is widely known as Iran's reformist president. He was elected by a landslide after a campaign that emphasized social reform, democracy, and a conciliatory foreign policy. Khatami's tenure as president saw some loosening of social restrictions and censorship, and some improvement took place in the economy and foreign relations. However, he faced deadlocks with conservatives on many issues and was harshly criticized by more radical reformers for failing to bring about more significant change. Many ordinary Iranians, more worried by inadequate economic progress than by lack of significant social reform, were also disillusioned with Khatami's lack of success.

In the 2005 presidential elections, to the surprise of many, **Mahmoud Ahmadinejad**, mayor of Tehran, rose to prominence and defeated Rafsanjani to become the Islamic Republic's sixth president. Ahmadinejad ran on a platform that opposed government corruption, promised economic benefits to Iran's lower classes, and touted a return to the Islamic populist values of the revolution, though his positions on Iran's nuclear program, Israel, and the Holocaust have brought him notoriety abroad (see chapter 4). Since coming to power Ahmadinejad has encountered opposition from a variety of sources within Iran. He experienced difficulty obtaining parliamentary approval for his cabinet nominations, and prominent Iranian economists have argued that his populist fiscal policies will have negative long-term effects on the economy. Conservatives have criticized Ahmadinejad for failing to maintain a hard line on social issues such as the veiling of women, and pragmatists have objected to his inflammatory statements that further antagonize the West against Iran. Presidential elections are slated for late spring of 2009, and only time will tell whether Ahmadinejad has retained the support base that initially brought him to power.

Supreme Leader

Even prior to Khomeini's death it was widely recognized that no successor to the post of supreme leader would possess the aura of authority and unique charisma of the leader of the revolution. Thus the appointment of **Ali Khamanei** as supreme leader represented a shift in the country's leadership, in particular because Khamanei, unlike his predecessor, is better known for his political qualifications than for his religious expertise. As supreme leader, Khamanei is the single most influential entity in the Iranian government and has the last word on every political issue facing the country. In practice, however, he does not regularly intervene directly in the day-to-day workings of the government. Described as a cautious administrator with an eye for detail, Khamanei is a social conservative who encourages scientific progress and economic privatization. He has emphasized the importance of women's and human rights, but he conceptualizes these rights within a semi-conservative Shi'a Islamic framework that many in the international community find unsatisfactory. The post of supreme leader is a lifetime appointment, and upon Khamanei's death the Assembly of Experts will again be responsible for choosing Iran's next supreme leader.

ECONOMY

Western media coverage of Iran tends to be dominated by reports on the country's nuclear program, the statements of various leaders regarding Israel, and human rights issues. These are also concerns within Iran, but for most Iranians they rank well behind the importance of another issue: the economy.

Iran faced a variety of economic challenges prior to the revolution, and the tremendous income gap between the wealthy few and the remainder of society was a source of resentment for Iran's many poor. Consequently, implementing a just economic system was one of the goals of the revolution. The tumultuous events of the revolution, however, threw the country's economy into a state of disarray that was quickly exacerbated by war, sanctions, fluctuating oil prices, and internal disagreement on economic policy. In the decades since, Iran's economy has experienced growth in a number of areas despite these factors,

Industry and Agriculture in Iran

Iran's arable land is spread across a variety of climactic zones, allowing the growth of a wide variety of crops. Between 10 and 15 percent of Iran's total area is under cultivation, with common crops including wheat and rice, a wide range of fruits and vegetables, sugar cane, sugar beets, cotton, nuts, and spices. Many of the world's pistachios are grown in Iran, which also produces most of the world's saffron. Livestock and poultry are raised for meat, dairy products, eggs, and wool, and fishing, particularly on the Caspian Sea, is the source of large amounts of caviar sold on the domestic and international markets.

Iran's industrial sector is dominated by petroleum, and the country also has a booming natural gas industry. The petrochemical and heavy metals industries are also substantial. Other prosperous industries include fertilizers, construction materials (particularly cement), textiles, and food processing (especially of sugar and vegetable oils).

Tomb of the Persian poet Sa'adi in Shiraz.

The Arts and Iran: Literature

Iran boasts one of the world's oldest and most influential literary traditions, which originated in ancient Persian civilization and went on to shape and be shaped by Islamic thought and culture. The bulk of Persian literature has taken the form of poetry, and the father of classical Persian poetry is Ferdowsi, whose epic *Shahnameh* (Book of Kings) traces the mythical path of Persian history from the creation of the world to the seventh-century Islamic conquest. Other literary giants include Sa'adi, Rumi, and Hafiz, whose works are rooted in mystical Islamic spirituality, also known as Sufism. In the nineteenth century Iranian writers and poets began to be influenced by western literary forms, and novels and short stories written in Persian appeared for the first time in the twentieth century. Such influence has been a two-way street, with western poets ranging from Goethe to Ralph Waldo Emerson citing the inspiration of Persian poetry in

(continued on next page)

but it continues to face many problems, in particular an overarching dependency on oil that no government has yet been able to shake.

Iranian desires for economic justice have manifested themselves in a variety of ways in the country's politics. Following the revolution, the Islamic government was mired in a series of debates concerning the economic path the country should take. Many revolutionaries had an Islamic leftist vision for economic reform that emphasized concern for the poor and the elimination of economic oppression. This vision was influential in the state takeover of much of the economy throughout the early 1980s, and it led to a closing of the income gap soon after the revolution, in spite of overall economic decline. Many, however, believed that the leftist economic policies of the 1980s were unsustainable and incompatible with Islamic law, which safeguards private property and upholds individual contractual rights.

By the end of the 1980s, devastated by war and fluctuating oil prices, the Iranian economy was in crisis. This led many in the government to support moves toward privatization and a free market economy. This movement is still in progress, but it has encountered difficulty from a number of sides. Along with privatization has come a renewal of the income distribution gap, and inflation and unemployment continue to affect the lives of many Iranians. Iran's poor are economically better off than they were prior to the revolution, primarily due to heavy government expenditure in healthcare and education as well as a successful movement to provide better services and living conditions in rural areas. The ability of the poor to make ends meet, however, depends on large-scale government subsidies of basic commodities including foodstuffs and gasoline. Proponents of a free-market economy advocate the end of such subsidies, but revoking them threatens to erode the support of the common people for the government. Leftist and populist slogans continue to hold the power to sway Iranian votes, as was evidenced by the appeal of Ahmadinejad's campaign promises to place the country's oil money in the hands of the people and return to the revolutionary values related to economic justice. It is likely that economic issues will play a vital role in Iranian politics for some time, and Iranian officials will continue to face the complex challenges of global and domestic economic realities as well as their people's expectations of economic justice and stability.

SOCIETY

Demographic Changes

Iranian society has undergone a number of demographic changes in recent decades. During the time of the shah the rural population began to migrate to urban areas in search of employment, and this trend continued after the revolution, with the result that the majority of Iranians now live in urban environments. This urbanization along with greatly improved levels of education has changed traditional patterns of Iranian life and resulted in a modernization of the cultural landscape of the country.

Iran also experienced a population growth spurt in the decade following the revolution, when the political leadership encouraged Iranians to have large families. The stress of such a policy on the country's resources soon became apparent, and at the end of the 1980s the government began to encourage lower birth rates through a remarkably well-funded, efficient, and effective family planning network that provides Iranians with birth control and reproductive education and counseling. As a result, birth rates have dropped dramatically, and population growth rates resemble those of the United States. The current president, Mahmoud Ahmadinejad, has deviated from the policy of encouraging small family sizes, but it remains to be seen whether this will have any effect on the family planning programs in place.

A fresco in Chehel Sutun Palace, Esfahan.

their work. Victorian audiences raved over Edward Fitzgerald's translation of Omar Khayyam's *Rubaiyat*, and in more recent times Coleman Barks' translations of Rumi's poetry have made bestseller lists. Literature has always been an important part of Iranian culture, and present-day Iran boasts a lively literary scene. Iranians generally display a remarkable knowledge of literature, and Persian-speakers of all walks of life often weave well-known couplets from their poetic heritage into everyday conversation.

The Arts and Iran: Persian Miniatures

The most well-known form of Iranian painting is the miniature. This art form became popular in Persia in the thirteenth century, reaching its height in the fifteenth and sixteenth centuries. The style of Persian miniatures was influenced by Byzantine illuminated manuscripts as well as by Chinese paintings, and miniatures were most often used to illustrate literary texts. The subjects of Persian paintings include bird and flower motifs as well as mythical, religious, and love scenes depicted in bright colors and surprising amounts of detail. The miniature tradition shapes much of modern Persian painting, including that of Mahmoud Farshchian, a prominent Iranian artist whose work has earned him fame in his own country and substantial recognition abroad.

Changes in Rural Areas

Life in the rural areas of Iran long revolved around patterns of subsistence agriculture or, in the cases of nomadic tribes, the transient grazing patterns of livestock. Due to a number of factors, including changes in farming techniques, changing economic conditions, and policies enacted by the Pahlavis and the post-revolutionary government, these patterns have changed drastically over the course of the last century. In the 1960s Iran was nearly self-sufficient in food production, but by the time of the revolution the country imported at least two-thirds of its food from abroad, and unemployed agricultural workers flocked to the cities in droves. The Islamic republic prioritized agricultural self-sufficiency and initiated a shift toward commercial farming but was unable to make significant progress in this area until the 1990s. Currently Iran is self-sufficient in most essential food commodities, and agricultural products make up a healthy share of its non-oil exports.

Agricultural developments and government-sponsored efforts have changed the rural landscape of Iran since the revolution. Prior to 1979, living conditions in many of Iran's rural areas were characterized by deprivation, and few of the country's rural inhabitants had access to healthcare, education, and basic infrastructural services. The post-revolutionary government, in a movement known as the Construction Jihad, brought health clinics, schools, roads, electricity, piped water, and other services to many of the country's far-flung provinces. Many of Iran's rural areas continue to face problems related to agriculture and income generation, and poverty remains a reality for rural inhabitants in some provinces, but the general improvement in conditions over the last several decades is remarkable.

Health

Another area in which Iran has made tremendous strides since the revolution is the field of healthcare. Prior to the revolution Iran faced a serious shortage of healthcare professionals, and many people had virtually no access to basic healthcare. The constitution of the Islamic republic guaranteed Iranian citizens access to adequate medical care, and shortly after the revolution the government pursued an aggressive policy of training health care professionals, building public clinics and hospitals, and implementing a universal healthcare system. Questions have been raised in some cases about quality of care and the expertise of health care personnel, and some worry that economic hardship coupled with population growth may impact the government's ability to meet future healthcare needs of its citizens. The healthcare system also continues to face challenges in combating malnutrition and communicable diseases as well as rising instances of drug addiction that have fueled an increased risk of HIV infection, though HIV prevalence is still fairly low by international standards.

Despite these concerns, the overall improvement in the population's health since the revolution is impressive. Maternal, infant, and child mortality rates have decreased drastically, and life expectancy has risen. Most pharmaceutical products used in Iran are produced within the country and provided to the public at affordable prices made possible by government subsidies. Over 90 percent of Iranians have access to safe drinking water—a far higher percentage than other countries in the region. These and other statistics are a testament to the good record of the Islamic republic in providing healthcare to its citizens.

Education

Education and literacy levels in Iran have risen sharply in the decades since the revolution due to extensive government investment in education. The revolutionary government instituted a complete overhaul of Iran's education system, including rewriting of curriculum according to Islamic guidelines. Schools have been built in all areas of Iran, and student-teacher ratios are

The Arts and Iran: Handicrafts

Iran has a lively handicraft tradition, with some of the most famous arts including metal engraving, inlay, enamelwork, weaving, and cloth stamping (shown above). Iran has one of the world's most impressive collections of royal jewelry, and the crown jewels of past Iranian dynasties can be seen on display in Tehran. Other handicrafts are showcased in Iran's many architectural masterpieces, which are ornamented with handmade tiles and mirror work. The handicraft for which Iran is most famous, however, is carpet weaving. The art of hand-woven and -knotted carpets in Persia dates back well over two thousand years, and carpets vary in size, design, and quality according to the skill and culture of the weaver. Most carpets are made of wool, but silk and cotton are also used. Handmade carpets remain a prominent export of Iran despite market difficulties experienced as a result of sanctions and political issues as well as growing competition from other countries producing handmade rugs.

An Iranian television reporter with members of an MCC learning tour in the background.

The Arts and Iran: Cinema

In recent decades Iran has made a name in the film industry, with Iranian directors winning international acclaim for their work. In 1997 filmmaker Abbas Kiarostami won the prestigious *Palme d'Or* at the Cannes Film Festival for his work *Taste of Cherry*, and other outstanding Iranian films have also received awards both at home and abroad. The subjects of Iranian art films are often common people who find hope and joy amidst the hardship and despair of life. Children figure prominently in many notable movies, particularly the beautiful films of director Majid Majidi. See the resources section for films subtitled in English and readily available to North American audiences.

generally good. Women in particular have benefited from improvements in the educational system, as evidenced by drastically increased literacy rates (approximately one-third of Iranian women were literate in the late 1970s, as compared to three-fourths today) and the disproportionately high number of female students in the university system. Male literacy rates have also risen dramatically and continue to be slightly higher than those for females.

Public education in Iran is divided into four levels: primary school, middle school, secondary school, and university. Attendance through middle school is compulsory, and all education prior to university level is gender-segregated. Most universities are co-educational, and students pay only nominal fees, though they are expected to spend time in government service following graduation. The competition for entrance into the public university system is stiff, with several million students competing for several hundred thousand places each year. The process for entrance into private universities and technical, vocational, and community colleges is less rigorous. A major problem faced by Iranian university students is a lack of employment options available after graduation. This has resulted in a phenomenon known as "brain drain," in which highly educated persons emigrate to find work abroad.

The university system in Iran underwent a period of considerable turmoil following the revolution when the new government instituted a "cultural revolution" designed to bring Islamic values to the Iranian academy and purge it of professors and students with leftist and Western leanings. Iran's institutions of higher education were closed for two years, and many intellectuals left the country during that time. Those who remained within the system were expected to conform to a government-approved Islamic ideology. In the years since, the government has continued to impose certain boundaries on academic freedom, but recent years have seen vibrant intellectual endeavor. Both the university and the religious seminary system are forums for quality research and the lively debate of various ideologies. Scholarly activities such as the translation of foreign-language sources and publication of high-quality academic journals are also flourishing.

Women's Issues

The cultural and political changes of the last century have transformed the place of women in Iranian society. As Iran entered the modern period under the Qajar dynasty, the situation of women varied widely according to economic class and social status. In towns and cities women generally occupied the domestic sphere, and heavy veiling and segregation of the sexes was the norm. Rural and nomadic women tended to veil less stringently (if at all) and have greater freedom of movement and activity outside the home, but they often lived a harsher existence. Generally, however, and much like women in western societies of the same era, Iranian women had less power than the men in their communities and were granted fewer rights by religious and civil laws.

As the upper and middle classes began to experience westernization in the final decades of the Qajar period, some of the restrictions on women began to be loosened, particularly in urban environments. In the 1920s and 30s women began tentatively entering the work force, and a fledgling women's movement emerged. The emancipation of women was part and parcel of the Pahlavi vision of modernization, but both Reza and Muhammad Shahs' disregard for Islamic family values and societal gender norms put them at odds with the conservative, traditionalist majority of Iranians. Reza Shah's attempts to forcibly unveil Iranian women proved disastrous (see sidebar on veiling in Iran on page 33), but his efforts and those of his son to educate women and bring them into the workforce were somewhat more successful. In 1963, women were granted the right to vote, and 1975 saw the passage, at the shah's behest, of a Family Protection Law, the intent of which was to reform sharia-based family, marriage, and divorce laws. Ultimately, however, the changes introduced from above by the Pahlavi shahs had only small repercussions on the lives of women outside of the urban middle and upper classes.

Women turned out en masse to support the Islamic Revolution of 1979, and it has been widely observed that the major role they played served to empower Iranian women as a class and awaken among them a realization of their ability to bring about political and societal change. The participation of women in political movements was not new; women had been active in both the Tobacco Revolution and the Constitutional Revolution. But never had so many women, especially

Top: Chador-clad women walk in the courtyard of Jami'at al-Zahra, an all-female Shi'a seminary in Qom.

Bottom: Schoolchildren sit on a bench in an Esfahan park.

among the popular classes, involved themselves so publicly in the affairs of their country.

The years since the revolution have seen both improvements and setbacks in women's rights and the overall situation of Iran's women. The Iranian constitution guarantees women full rights in accordance with Islamic standards, but such standards can be interpreted in a variety of ways. Shortly after the revolution, the Islamic government revoked the shah's Family Protection Law and implemented laws that are widely seen by the West and some within Iran as discriminatory to women. Among other things these laws allow men more freedom and power than women to divorce their spouses, grant child custody to fathers in many or most cases, enforce veiling, and allow polygamy.

Despite shortcomings in existing laws and remaining cultural inequities, the overall situation of women in Iran has improved in many ways since the revolution, and it compares favorably to that of women in other countries in the region. The decades since the revolution have seen a rise in the number of women's organizations from across the ideological spectrum. Women have carved out a space for themselves in Iranian politics, winning seats in parliamentary elections, and being appointed to a variety of governmental posts. Divorce and custody laws have been reformed as women and men have worked from inside and outside the political system to effect change, and laws passed shortly after the revolution that barred women from various professions have since been revoked, allowing women to pursue all occupations other than that of courtroom judge. Advances in healthcare and education have particularly benefited women, and the dramatic rise in women's literacy and educational levels as well as the entrance of women into the work force in unprecedented levels has helped to remedy some imbalances of power. The entrance of women into the Islamic seminary system has also brought change, in some cases leading to religiously educated women arguing for cultural and legal changes that they consider both congruent with Islam and beneficial to women and society as a whole.

Western discussions of women's issues in Iran often ignore positive changes in the status of women that have occurred since the revolution. Furthermore, the cultural and economic factors contributing to the difficulties of many women are often overlooked, while Islam and the Islamic government are sometimes portrayed as the source of all ills. Such simplistic perspectives fail to take into account the many factors that shape the position of women in a given society, and the politicization of women's issues, both inside and outside of Iran, can overshadow the fact that tremendous diversity exists in Iranian women's situations, experiences, beliefs, and aspirations.

Many in Iran wish to improve the situation of women in their own society but do not readily embrace western conceptions of women's rights and freedoms. Iranians often point to aspects of western societies' treatment of women that they find deeply troubling, particularly the hyper-sexualized portrayals of women in media. And many Iranian women do not frame their concerns as gender issues but rather as broader human desires for physical, emotional, and spiritual well-being; economic security; and healthy relationships. Any western examination of the status of women in Iran should be informed by the recognition that problems pertaining to women also exist in the West, and the ability of Iranian women to determine priorities and shape issues for themselves should always be acknowledged.

Family and Social Life

Iranian views on family and social life have evolved in significant ways in recent decades, but they remain fairly conservative and informed by Islamic mores and traditional ways of life. An individual's life typically revolves around that of his or her family, and high priority is placed on maintaining a stable

Top: Family on a motorcycle, Tehran.

Bottom: Preschoolers line up for an outing to the park.

family structure and the proper upbringing of children. Paradigms of child-rearing have evolved, with current wisdom preferring a kind approach over the autocratic tendencies of previous generations. Iranian parents of both genders tend to be heavily involved in their children's education and care, particularly in the middle and upper classes, and adolescents and young adults are generally given more freedom to choose their own life course than they had been previously. Marriage patterns have also changed as educational endeavors and economic realities have prompted young people to marry at later ages. Heavy parental involvement in the selection of one's spouse is the norm, but young men and women are nearly always free to reject marriage proposals that do not suit them. Conceptions of gender roles have also evolved as many Iranian women, particularly in the middle and upper classes, have entered the work force.

In recent decades Iranian youth have had great influence on larger society. Student activism has long been strong in the country's universities, and it was a contributing factor to the Iranian revolution. A minimum voting age of fifteen put into place after the revolution gave young people across the country political clout (the voting age was raised to eighteen in early 2007). Student movements were instrumental in the election of reformist president Muhammad Khatami,

and young people have long been advocates of greater social freedom. Many of Iran's youth are highly motivated to succeed and pursue higher education and achievement aggressively, but find their efforts stymied by the difficulties of admission into a university and finding stable employment. In addition, many Iranians are gravely troubled by rising rates of drug addiction among the youth.

Technology has also been instrumental in changing the social landscape of Iran. Radio, film and television (in many cases satellite television) figure largely into Iranians' daily lives. Video games are popular with the youth, and computer and internet use have exploded over the past decade. Many Iranians have internet access in their homes, workplaces, and schools, and internet cafes are common in cities and towns. Government censorship of the internet exists, but tends to be limited to websites with pornographic, anti-Shi'a, and anti-government content. Blogging has become an increasingly popular forum for social interaction and the communication of ideas in Iran, and hundreds of thousands of Farsi-language blogs can be found on the internet.

The resource section located at the back of the book provides a starting point for those wishing to learn more about the topics summarized above as well as other aspects of Iranian history, society, and culture.

A busy Tehran sidewalk.

Iran and the West
Since 1979

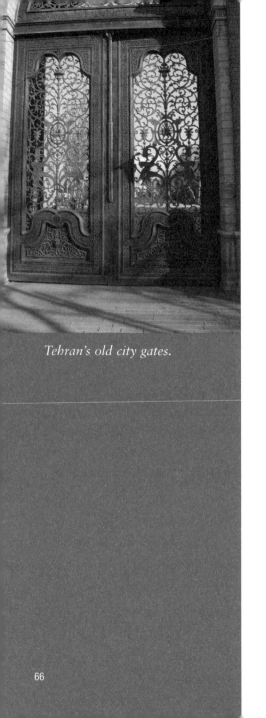

Tehran's old city gates.

4. Iran and the West Since 1979: Responses to Common Questions

This chapter lists some of the questions about Iran commonly asked by people in the churches in Canada and the United States that support Mennonite Central Committee (MCC) and its work in Iran. These questions are often shaped by mainstream media reports on current political issues and tensions between the Iranian government and the leadership of various western countries, particularly the United States. Accordingly, this chapter focuses primarily on Iranian-western political relations since the Islamic Revolution of 1979. Questions are arranged chronologically by topic, and responses attempt to provide as helpful an overview as possible of the complex subjects raised. Much of the following information highlights the tension that has characterized those relations, but it is important to note that the same time period has seen much positive non-political interaction between a variety of Iranian and western individuals and groups.

What was the hostage crisis?

On November 4, 1979, shortly after the U.S. government decided to allow ex-shah Muhammad Pahlavi into the United States to seek cancer treatment, a group of Iranian students occupied the U.S. Embassy in Tehran and held fifty-two American diplomats hostage until January 20, 1981. U.S. support of the shah had long been a key source of resentment for Iranians, particularly in light of the 1953 CIA-backed coup that deposed the democratically elected government of Mossadeq and reinstated the shah. Thus the ex-shah's entry into the United States reinforced the revolutionaries' fears that the U.S. government was planning to topple the revolutionary government and reinstate the monarchy.

The hostage crisis strengthened the more radical voices of the revolution and undermined the relatively more moderate factions. It appears that Ayatollah Khomeini was not aware of plans to take over the embassy until after the fact. Ultimately, however, Khomeini welcomed the development, though he warned the hostage-takers that no harm must come to any of the hostages. Initially sixty-six people were taken hostage, but the students quickly released women and African-Americans, citing Islam's regard of women and their own solidarity with oppressed minorities. Months later an additional hostage was released when he was diagnosed with multiple sclerosis.

Iran's conditions for release of the hostages included apologizing for American interference in Iranian affairs (in particular in the 1953 coup), releasing Iranian assets frozen by the United States, and returning the ex-shah to Iran for trial. President Jimmy Carter rejected these demands, instead approving a plan for a secret military rescue in April 1980. The rescue attempt was aborted in the Iranian desert due to mechanical failures and adverse weather conditions, and an ill-fated helicopter crash ended in the deaths of eight U.S. servicemen, all of which was taken by Iranians as an act of God.

The botched rescue attempt inclined the United States toward seeking a diplomatic solution, and the death of the ex-shah and invasion by Iraq, both of which occurred in the summer of 1980, made Iranian officials more willing to compromise. After a series of negotiations, an accord was reached between the two nations. Iran agreed to release the hostages in exchange for the release of eight billion dollars of Iranian assets and the guarantee that the U.S. would no longer intervene in the internal affairs of Iran in any way. The hostages were released on January 20, 1981, after 444 days in captivity.

Top: A man relaxes at the Shah Mosque in Esfahan.

Bottom: A school group enjoys the sunshine in a park in Esfahan.

Top: *An Iranian couple visiting Qom to pay homage at the shrine of Lady Fatima Ma'sumeh.*

Bottom: *Traditional musicians in Tehran.*

What was the involvement of the United States and other western countries in the Iran-Iraq war?

The support given Iraq by the United States and other western governments during the Iran-Iraq war was a source of tremendous political tension between Tehran and the West. The U.S. administration of Ronald Reagan, at odds with the revolutionary government in Iran, looked the other way when Iraq invaded Iran and later provided intelligence and military and economic aid to Saddam Hussein's Ba'ath regime. The United States also made great efforts through a campaign called Operation Staunch to block international sales of weaponry to Iran, while Iraq remained free to purchase military supplies on the international market throughout the course of the war. Perhaps the most controversial aspect of the international community's support of Iraq was the provision of supplies and knowledge related to chemical warfare. Both private companies and government entities in the United States, Germany, and the Netherlands, among others, helped Saddam Hussein develop chemical warfare capability, which he used extensively against Iran and Kurdish civilians in his own country. The lack of major international outcry against the use of chemical weapons by Iraq against Iran and the continued support by western powers of Saddam Hussein following the use of such weapons only confirmed Iranians' feelings that injustice and double standards typify the political stances of western governments against Iran.

In the last years of the Iran-Iraq war, the United States was drawn into military involvement in the conflict when Iran, in response to frequent Iraqi attacks on Iranian tankers, struck Kuwaiti oil tankers flying the U.S. flag. The bulk of U.S. military action entailed attacks on Iranian oil platforms, ships, and gunboats. Most tragically, this involvement included the shooting down of Iran Air Flight 655 by the USS *Vincennes*. Iranians were outraged by the deaths of the 290 civilians on board, as well as by the fact that the ship in question was in Iranian territorial waters at the time.

What was the Iran-Contra Affair?

Though the United States generally supported Iraq throughout the course of the war, officials in the Reagan administration, assisted in part by Israel, secretly sold arms to Iran for several years in the mid-1980s. These actions were at least partially motivated by a desire to prolong the conflict, thereby keeping two potentially dangerous foes (Iran and Iraq) occupied with one another. This became known as the Iran-Contra affair, because money from the sales was channeled to right-wing Contra guerillas who opposed the leftist, democratically elected, Sandinista government of Nicaragua. Both the sale of weapons and funding of the Contras were in violation of U.S. government policy and legislation. The Reagan administration also sought to use arms sales to Iran to induce Tehran to pressure Shi'a militant groups in Lebanon to release hostages taken during the Lebanese civil war, but this effort was largely unsuccessful.

What sanctions and punitive financial measures have been imposed on Iran?

Since the Islamic Revolution, the United States has imposed a variety of unilateral sanctions against Iran and pushed for the adoption of similar measures in the international sphere.

In the wake of the hostage crisis, the U.S. froze billions of dollars of Iranian assets. Some of these assets were released following resolution of the crisis, but a disputed amount remains frozen and is a source of contention between the U.S. and Iran. The U.S. also imposed wide-ranging unilateral sanctions throughout the course of the Iran-Iraq war. These sanctions were strengthened under the Clinton administration, which prohibited most commercial and financial dealings with Iran in 1995. The following year, Congress passed the Iran and Libya Sanctions Act (ILSA), which upheld the restrictions put in place the previous year and also imposed sanctions on foreign companies with significant investments in Iran's petroleum industry. The United States loosened sanctions slightly following the election of reformist president Muhammad Khatami, but Congress renewed the ILSA in 2001. Further sanctions, including some related to academic and scientific cooperation, have been imposed since that time by the United States Department of the Treasury.

More recently, the United Nations Security Council, under great pressure by the United States, imposed sanctions on Iran for failing to give up its uranium enrichment program in accordance with U.N. Resolution 1696. Resolutions 1737 and 1747, passed in

A mural on the side of a building in Tehran depicts Mary and the infant Jesus, both of whom are revered in Islam as well as Christianity.

December 2006 and March 2007, place financial restrictions on dealings related to Iran's nuclear program and individuals associated with it. Some have contested the legitimacy of these resolutions because Resolution 1696 calls on Iran to give up activities within its rights as a signatory to the Nuclear Non-Proliferation Treaty. In August 2008, the U.N. Security Council announced plans to impose new sanctions on Iran as the result of Iran's refusal to respond to its ultimatum to freeze uranium enrichment at current levels.

What is Iran's human rights record?

Iran is heavily criticized in the international arena for human rights abuses, particularly in the areas of women's issues, minority rights and freedom of the press, speech, and religion.

Many Iranians involved in the Islamic Revolution emphasized the importance of human rights, and the constitution adopted in 1979 and amended in 1989 grants citizens of Iran a wide range of rights including equal status before the law; protection of human, political, economic, social, and cultural rights; freedom of opinion; and freedom of the press. These rights, however, are understood within the framework of traditional interpretations of Islamic law, which differ substantially from secular, western constructs of human rights. Additionally, Iranian law contains vague, sweeping clauses that have been used by the judiciary to qualify the rights outlined in the constitution, particularly freedom of speech, freedom of religion, and freedom of the press. Journalists, political activists, and members of various religious or other groups are often prosecuted under charges such as insulting Islam, harming national security, inciting public opinion, and weakening the system.

Iranian law also contains specific provisions that are at odds with international conceptions of gender rights, sexual rights, religious rights, punishment, and retribution. The legal system treats men and women differently in regards to inheritance, divorce, child custody, and other issues. Since the revolution, important moves have been made toward more equitable treatment of women, but many laws and practices continue to spark criticism from women's rights activists both inside and outside the country. Homosexual activity, adultery, and other sexual conduct that violates Islamic norms are also prohibited by law, and those in violation of these laws are at times subject to harsh punishment.

Likewise, Iranian law limits certain religious rights in accordance with traditional interpretations of Islamic law. The right to practice religions other than Zoroastrianism, Judaism, Christianity, and Islam is not recognized, and the proselytizing of faiths other than Islam is illegal. Open apostasy from Islam is also against the law. Under these laws, adherents of faiths other than Islam can be prosecuted for evangelization, as can Muslims who convert to another religion.

Punishments meted out by Iranian courts also draw criticism from international human rights groups, in particular capital punishment (including public executions), the execution of individuals under age eighteen, and corporal punishment such as flogging. Human rights abuses such as false arrests, fraudulent convictions, extra-judicial killings, and the

physical abuse and torture of prisoners have also occurred. These abuses violate Iranian law, and their perpetrators have at times been brought to justice.

Many allegations of human rights abuses are disputed by the Iranian government, and conflicting narratives of specific events as well as lack of access by neutral third parties make some human rights violations difficult to verify. In some cases, accusations of human rights abuses have been fabricated or greatly exaggerated. The need for drastic reform, however, is recognized not only in the international arena, but also by a wide array of individuals and groups working within Iran. Some of these groups have adopted secular formulations of human rights, but far more approach the subject from within the framework of Islam. Human rights has been a subject of lively debate in the Islamic world for some time, and Muslim scholars and activists are continually working to develop new theories of human rights that are both suited to the modern world and congruent with the principles of Islam.

Outside criticism of human rights abuses in Iran should take into account the progress made by the country since the years immediately following the revolution as well as the fact that the human rights situation in Iran compares favorably with that of many of its neighbors, including some allies of the United States. Also worthy of consideration is

A young boy stands outside a mosque, where worshippers remove their shoes before entering.

a criticism levied by a variety of countries including Iran that international organizations such as the United Nations adopt human rights standards that fail to take into account the cultural norms and religious values of non-Western countries. Iran has also decried the double standards of the international community, pointing out that the U.S., which strongly criticizes the Iranian regime, overlooked violations that took place under the rule of the shah and is itself guilty of violating international human rights conventions.

What is Iran's nuclear program? How should the international community respond?

A TIMELINE OF IRAN'S NUCLEAR PROGRAM

Iran's nuclear program began during the reign of Muhammad Pahlavi, when the Tehran Nuclear Research Center was opened in 1967 with the assistance of a U.S. government program called "Atoms for Peace." A short time later, Iran signed the Nuclear Non-Proliferation Treaty (NPT) at its inception in 1968. The Shah calculated that Iran could earn and invest far more from exporting its carbon resources than from subsidizing their consumption at home, and until the fall of his regime he was supported by the United States in his ambition to attain a complete nuclear fuel cycle. Following the Islamic Revolution, the country's nuclear program fell into disarray. Many of its major components were cancelled either by Iran or its international nuclear partners, and nuclear sites were a frequent target of Iraqi bombing campaigns during the course of the Iran-Iraq war.

Once the war was over, the Iranian government re-started its nuclear energy program, though on a smaller scale than in the time of the shah. Throughout the early 1990s Iran partnered with Russia, China, Germany, and other countries to further its nuclear program, citing the desire that 20 percent of the country's energy be produced by nuclear power by the year 2005. After the revolution, the United States' position on Iran's nuclear energy program changed, and it began taking active steps to dissuade other countries' cooperation with the Islamic republic. In the early parts of the decade, Tehran was accused of developing nuclear weapons. In response, in 1992 and 1993 the International Atomic Energy Association (IAEA) made a series of visits to Iran's nuclear facilities. Following these and other visits over the course of the decade, the IAEA declared that the sites visited and activities witnessed were consistent with peaceful purposes, though it called some visits inconclusive.

In 2002, a member of an Iranian dissident group publicized the existence of uranium enrichment and heavy water facilities that Iran had failed to disclose to the IAEA. As a result, France, Germany, and the United Kingdom, known as the EU-3, opened a diplomatic initiative with Iran in relation to its nuclear program. Iran agreed to suspend the enrichment and reprocessing of uranium and signed an "additional protocol" to the NPT, which allowed for closer IAEA monitoring of its nuclear program. After subsequent inspections, the IAEA reported in November 2003 that Iran had engaged in a "pattern of concealment" in its nuclear activities, though it also reported that it found no evidence that Iran's activities were related to a nuclear weapons development program. The United States, however, maintained that Iran was actively pursuing the acquisition of weapons of mass destruction. In May 2003 Iran sent a letter to the United States offering to engage in a wide-ranging dialogue on subjects including nuclear cooperation, termination of aid to Palestinian militants, and recognition of Israel. The United States did not respond.

In 2004, the IAEA expressed disappointment that Iran had not suspended all uranium-enrichment activities and adopted a resolution calling on Iran to do so. After subsequent negotiations

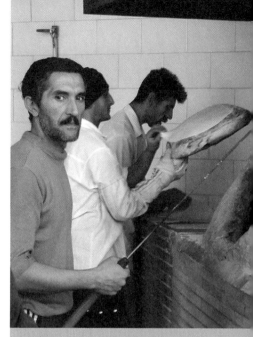

Bakers work in an Esfahan bread shop typical of the many that appear on street corners across Iran. The flat bread known as lavash *is a staple for many Iranians.*

Top: The famous Si-o-Seh bridge in Esfahan.

Bottom: The arches of the bridge as seen from beneath.

between Iran and the EU-3, Iran voluntarily agreed to suspend most enrichment for a limited period of time. In 2005, Iran announced its intentions to resume enrichment activities despite IAEA and EU-3 urgings to the contrary, and it went on to remove IAEA seals at various enrichment sites.

In January 2006, following the resumption of enrichment activities, the IAEA and EU-3 released a statement saying that Iran's actions amounted to a rejection of the diplomatic process, and in February the IAEA referred Iran to the Security Council. On April 11, 2006, Iranian President Mahmoud Ahmadinejad announced that Iran had successfully enriched uranium, calling on the world to recognize Iran's right under the NPT to peaceful atomic technology.

In December 2006, the United Nations Security Council voted to impose sanctions on Iran for its refusal to cease enrichment activities, and in March 2007, the sanctions were strengthened. In October 2007, the United States imposed further unilateral sanctions on Iran. Throughout 2007 and the first half of 2008, Iran worked with the IAEA to resolve questions about its nuclear activities, and the IAEA conducted fourteen unannounced visits.

An important development occurred in December 2007, when the United States National Intelligence Estimate stated that Iran had previously pursued the development of weapons of mass destruction, but that it had ceased its attempts in 2003. This prompted widespread calls by U.S. and European government officials and many others for the United States to completely overhaul its policies in relation to Iran and pursue direct, high-level negotiations. On May 26, 2008, the IAEA released a report documenting Iran's compliance with the nuclear watchdog's policies, though it stated that Iran had not yet provided necessary documentation on some outstanding issues, including allegations of nuclear weapons-related research.

July 2008 marked a thaw in U.S.-Iranian relations when the United States sent Undersecretary of State William Burns to sit in on a meeting between the European Union's foreign policy chief and Iran's top nuclear negotiator. The meeting was hampered by U.S. insistence that Iran cease to enrich uranium as a precondition to talks. Iran proposed continuing with talks but declined to freeze its enrichment program as requested, and the Security Council subsequently announced plans for new sanctions.

INTERNATIONAL CONCERN AND IRANIAN RESPONSES

The controversy over Iran's nuclear program has centered primarily on the country's uranium enrichment activities. Uranium enrichment is permitted under the NPT and is a vital component of a nuclear energy program. It is a matter of concern, however, because having the capability to enrich uranium to the low levels needed by a peaceful energy program puts a nation one major step closer to producing high enriched uranium, which is a crucial component in the production of nuclear weapons. The IAEA reports that Iran has enriched uranium only to low levels, but critics believe that even this capability in the hands of the Islamic Republic is a potential danger. Iran's past failures to disclose parts of its nuclear program to the IAEA have also been a source of concern, and the country's after-the-fact efforts to rectify these problems have done little to put to rest the worries of those who perceive Iran as a dire threat to the United States and Israel. IAEA reports also allege that Iran is doing nuclear weapons-related research and call upon Iran to address these allegations.

Responding to these issues, Iran has generally maintained that it has no intentions of building a weapon. Iranian leaders have pointed out many times that enriching uranium is within their rights under the NPT and have demanded that their right to do so be respected by the international community. They have also expressed their reticence to be dependent upon outside sources for a commodity indispensable to a nuclear power program. Leaders of the Islamic Republic have also remarked that it is hypocritical for countries that possess and have used nuclear weapons to speak of fearing a nuclear-armed Iran. Arguments defending Iran's actions also point out that Iran has in many cases submitted to IAEA inspections outside the scope of the agreements it has signed, and call into question the legitimacy of weapons research-related allegations, saying they are trumped up by neoconservatives in the U.S. government and pro-Israel lobby groups such as the American Israel Public Affairs Committee. Additionally, a non-aligned movement made up of over 120 countries has supported Iran's right to pursue peaceful nuclear energy and the full fuel cycle.

MILITARY ACTION VERSUS DIPLOMACY

Many neoconservatives in Washington as well as leaders in the Israeli government and members of the pro-Israel lobby in the U.S. believe that the only way to prevent Iran from acquiring weapons of mass destruction is for the U.S. (or Israel) to launch a military strike against its nuclear facilities. Many others, including those in the Anabaptist faith community, strongly oppose military action on principle or because they believe an attack on Iran would create more problems than it would solve. Even a limited attack could have great human cost and such an attack could easily mushroom into a larger and even more destructive regional conflict. Iranians seeking to reform their government from within, including Nobel Peace Prize-winning activist Shirin Ebadi, have spoken out against military strikes, saying that they could endanger their work for democratization and liberalization. An attack could cause Iranians, even those ambivalent about their own government, to adopt a siege mentality and rally to defend their country. This was certainly the case following Iraq's 1980 invasion of Iran, when Iranians displayed unity of purpose and a strong capacity for self-defense despite domestic political strife.

Even in the best-case scenario, a military strike would only deepen the climate of fear and suspicion that feeds the current conflicts in the Middle East and that is often a driving force behind nations' desires to arm themselves with the world's most destructive weapons. The United States' refusal to take the military option off the table and to engage in negotiations without preconditions has done little to encourage Iran to give up certain aspects of its nuclear program. Threats and pressure toward Iran have proven counterproductive, but taking a nonviolent approach to the resolution of this conflict could ratchet down the dangerous level of tension that characterizes the issue, allowing Iran, the United States, and others to come to the table and negotiate a solution in which the legitimate security concerns and national interests of all sides are addressed. Furthermore, those who support the assertive pursuit of diplomatic solutions point out the value of a regional approach to the issue of nuclear weapons, saying that a focus on Iran's nuclear program that ignores other realities in the region such as Israeli possession of weapons of mass destruction undermines the credibility of the international community and opens it to charges of hypocrisy.

Is Iran a threat to Israel?

"Death to Israel" was one of the main slogans of the Iranian Revolution of 1979, and since that time leaders of the Islamic Republic have repeatedly expressed their opposition to the state of Israel. President

Mahmoud Ahmadinejad has been highly criticized in the West for a speech he gave in October 2005 in which he quoted Ayatollah Khomeini's statement that Israel would "vanish from the page of time," also translated as "wiped off the map." Ahmadinejad has also been condemned for calling into question whether the Holocaust occurred.

These statements have led many to believe that Iran is a significant threat to Israel, and that in the event Iran acquired weapons of mass destruction, it would use them to strike the Jewish State. The antagonistic statements of Iran's leaders, however, must be considered alongside more measured, pragmatic stances they have simultaneously taken toward Israel. Both Supreme Leader Ayatollah Ali Khamanei and President Ahmadinejad have consistently maintained that they do not seek the military destruction of Israel. Instead, they have expressed their ideal that all the people of Palestine-Israel, whether Muslim, Jewish, or Christian, should be allowed to take part in a general referendum to select a democratic government that would preside over one inclusive state. They have also indicated on various occasions that Iran will accept any solution to the Palestinian-Israeli conflict that the Palestinians accept. In face-to-face meetings with Christian leaders from Canada and the United States in 2006 and 2007, President Ahmadinejad insisted that his statement that Israel would "vanish from the page of time" did not refer to military action, but to his belief that Israel, like the Soviet Union, will eventually dissolve from within due to inconsistencies in its policies. In those same meetings, when pressed on his remarks about the Holocaust, Ahmadinejad stressed that his concern was less with the Holocaust itself and more with the use of this event to justify Israeli expansionism and mistreatment of Palestinians.

Iran and Israel's ideological differences are substantial and unlikely to be resolved in the near future, but the past has shown

Rural landscapes on the road between Esfahan and Shiraz.

Shoppers in Qom's Arab Bazaar.

that it is possible for the two nations to coexist in peace despite these differences. In the 1980s, common concerns about Iraq and the Soviet Union prompted Iran and Israel to maintain a working, if uneasy, relationship despite Israeli opposition to the Khomeini government and Iranian anti-Israel rhetoric and support of Hezbollah. Current high levels of tension between the two countries may be rooted in a post-Cold War, post-Saddam Hussein rivalry for power and influence in the Middle East rather than in ideological differences or Iran's nuclear program.

Peace organizations including MCC encourage governments in the Middle East and beyond to take the lead in addressing the tension between Iran and Israel in the context of multilateral diplomatic negotiations, with the goal of forging a regional order that is based on mutual understanding and compromise and that respects the security needs of all parties involved. In order for such negotiations to take place, tension-heightening rhetoric and threats must cease, whether they come from Iranian leaders or from the Israeli government, which has persistently made threatening statements about attacking Iran and is known to possess several hundred nuclear weapons.

MCC also believes that making the Middle East a zone free from weapons of mass destruction is an important step in securing peace in the region. Additionally, any lasting peace in the Middle East hinges on a just and peaceful resolution to the Palestinian-Israeli conflict, and thus MCC and others have maintained that diplomatic negotiations to that end must be assertively pursued.

Is it true that the Iranian government supports terrorism?

The U.S. government labels Iran as a "state sponsor of terrorism," accusing Iran of encouraging anti-Israeli terrorism, providing assistance to insurgents in Iraq and Afghanistan, and having links to Al Qaeda. Many of these claims are disputed not only by Iran itself, but also by European allies of the United States as well as various officials within the U. S. government and military.

Iran openly supports organizations that oppose the Israeli occupation of Palestine, in particular Hezbollah, a Shi'a political, paramilitary, and social service organization operating inside Lebanon that has a history of resisting Israeli incursions into that country. Views on Hezbollah vary widely. The group is not considered a terrorist organization by the United Nations, though six countries (Australia, Canada, Israel, the Netherlands, the United Kingdom, and the United States) have designated either Hezbollah in its entirety or its military wing as such. In the Arab world and beyond, Hezbollah is viewed by many as a legitimate resistance organization. Iran has also supported Palestinian militant groups such as Hamas, though the extent and nature of that support remains a matter of debate.

Since the invasion of Iraq in 2003, the United States has repeatedly claimed that Iran has provided weapons and training to militant groups attacking U.S. soldiers in Iraq. Iran hotly contests this claim and points out that stability in Iraq is in its interests as well as those of the United States. Iraqi government officials have remarked that they have no conclusive evidence that Iran supports extremists in their country, reiterating that Iran and Iraq share common goals. For its own part, Iran has criticized the humanitarian consequences of the United States' invasion and occupation of Iraq in general as well as its actions in detaining Iranian diplomats in Iraq in 2006. Iran also claims that the United States is providing safe haven for the Mujahideen-e Khalq, which has widely been designated a terrorist organization for the many attacks it has carried out within Iran.

The United States has also claimed in recent years that Iran has provided support to the Taliban insurgency in Afghanistan.

Top: This small grocery in the village of Khaveh in the province of Qom is similar to tens of thousands of others in neighborhoods across Iran.

Bottom: A busy Tehran freeway.

The brightly lit minarets and gold dome of the Lady Fatima Ma'sumeh shrine stand out in a nighttime view of Qom's skyline.

Both U.N. and Afghan government officials have disputed this claim, pointing to Iran's ideological differences with extremist Sunni Muslims, history of opposing the Taliban, and extensive cooperation with the Afghan government in the areas of development and combating drug trafficking.

U.S. government officials have also linked Iran to Al Qaeda, saying that Iran has allowed members of Al Qaeda to operate from within its borders and in other cases refused to release members of Al Qaeda detained by Iran into the custody of other countries. However, Al Qaeda's strong anti-Shi'a and anti-Iranian orientation calls into question the validity of these claims. Iran vehemently denies granting Al Qaeda safe haven, citing the incompatibility between the conservative Shi'a Islam that forms the basis of the government of the Islamic Republic and the extremist interpretations of Sunni Islam to which Al Qaeda adheres.

When considering the issue of terrorism in the Middle East, the complex political, historical, and religious landscape of the region must be taken into account. The language of the "war on terror" has often blurred important differences in the histories, ideologies, strategies, and goals of various groups given the label "terrorist." The differences between these groups as well as the factors that motivate individuals to join them must be recognized and understood by all those who strive for just and peaceful resolutions to conflicts in the Middle East.

Bob Nalley (right), member of an MCC learning tour to Iran, converses with a young Iranian outside a building in Tehran.

Anabaptist Responses to Iran

Top: Houses destroyed by the earthquake in Bam.

Bottom: A mosque in Bam partially survived the destruction.

5. ANABAPTIST RESPONSES TO IRAN

I. Mennonite Involvement in Iran

Mennonites have been involved in Iran since the early 1990s. Mennonite and Brethren in Christ churches in Canada and the United States have provided humanitarian assistance through Mennonite Central Committee (MCC) in the midst of emergencies and in the aftermath of natural disasters. In addition, Mennonite individuals and institutions have responded to calls from within Christian and Muslim communities to work toward peace and justice in a time when Iranian-American, Iranian-Canadian, and Muslim-Christian relations are marred by hostility and lack of respect.

MCC INVOLVEMENT IN IRAN

MCC began its work in Iran following a 1990 earthquake that devastated the Gilan and Zanjan provinces of northeastern Iran. At that time a humanitarian partnership was forged between MCC and the Iranian Red Crescent Society (IRCS), a large-scale Islamic aid organization. Cooperation between MCC and the IRCS has continued up to the present time, with MCC contributing to the Red Crescent Society's work among Afghan and Iraqi refugees as well as its relief and reconstruction efforts following the December 2003 earthquake in Bam, which killed tens of thousands of Iranians and left many more homeless. Through this partnership, MCC and IRCS personnel have formed strong bonds rooted in the common ground of faith-based service. The partnership also paved the way for a student exchange program and other efforts that are part of an MCC key initiative.

MCC has cooperated with individuals and organizations of other faiths for many years, but in 2004 its International Programs department chose to consciously seek out such partnerships, making interfaith bridge building a programmatic key initiative for the next five years. MCC approaches interfaith bridge building primarily through the paradigm of building relationships and mutual service, recognizing that these are vital aspects of Christian witness and that they can lead to theological conversation, formal dialogue, and mutual transformation. Such was the case in 1998, when the MCC-IRCS partnership opened the doors to the formation of a Muslim-Christian exchange program. As part of this interfaith dialogue initiative, Mennonite Christians study Islam and Persian at the Imam Khomeini Education and Research Institute (IKERI) in Qom, Iran, and Iranian Shi'a Muslims study philosophy of religion in Canada at the University of Toronto with the cooperation of the Toronto Mennonite Theological Centre and Conrad Grebel University College.

In addition to the student exchange, conferences have also taken place in Ontario and Qom in which Mennonite Christian and Shi'a Muslim scholars and theologians have discussed topics such as tradition and modernity, revelation and authority, and spiritual practices. MCC has also sponsored Iranian attendance at the Summer Peacebuilding Institute of the Center for Justice and Peacebuilding at Eastern Mennonite University as well as conducting learning tours in which Mennonites from Canada and the United States travel to Iran to meet Iranians and learn about Persian history, society, and culture. Most recently, the exchange opened up the opportunity for religious leaders from the United States and Canada to meet four times with Iranian President Ahmadinejad. Three meetings took place in New York in 2006, 2007, and 2008, and in February 2007 religious leaders from the United States traveled to Iran in an effort to build friendship and goodwill. These meetings were noteworthy for the way in which participants engaged one another on religious grounds and broached difficult topics with mutual respect despite differences.

Members of an MCC learning tour to Iran stand outside the Imam Khomeini Education and Research Institute.

Keepers of Each Other's Dignity

Evie Shellenberger reflects on the time she and her husband Wally spent as participants in a Muslim-Christian exchange program between MCC and IKERI.

While in Iran we spent the month of Ramadan fasting alongside our Muslim friends. Several evenings each week we ended the day's fast by sharing a meal with various families. One evening we were guests in the home of some new acquaintances, where we sat together on the floor eating delicious saffron rice and Persian stew, trying hard to communicate in Farsi. We talked about why we were in Iran and what we hoped to gain from our student exchange experience. Our hostess commented that she understood some things about Christianity, but until we came to Iran she had never heard about Mennonites. "Who are Mennonites?" she asked. I was very much a beginner in the Farsi language and wondered how I would

(continued on next page)

Evie Shellenberger, participant in the Muslim-Christian exchange program sponsored by MCC and IKERI, converses with young women at the tomb of Hafiz in Shiraz.

ever be able to explain who the Mennonites are. A wonderful friend, Haydeh, sat next to me. Sensing my discomfort, she sat forward and said with passion, "I can tell you about the Mennonites. They are followers of Jesus who try to live according to the teachings of Jesus. They believe in peace and work in ninety countries all around the world helping needy people. In some countries they work closely with Muslims to help the poor." I listened to her kind and powerful words about a faith different from her own religion of Islam. It was a moment of transformation for me to experience someone from another religion explaining my own faith at its best. When I returned home, I wondered, would I be able to speak passionately and kindly about the strengths of Islam? Perhaps one important outcome of the exchange program is that Muslims and Christians can depend on one another to speak truthfully about faith issues and will be keepers on one another's dignity and pride.

In addition to its efforts to build peace across religious lines, MCC has engaged in political advocacy through its Washington office, discouraging military action against Iran and encouraging United States government officials to enter into comprehensive negotiations with Iran to address issues of dispute and to adopt policies that would improve trade and restore diplomatic relations between the two countries.

OTHER MENNONITE INITIATIVES

A variety of Mennonite organizations have participated directly in MCC peacebuilding initiatives related to Iran, including Mennonite Church USA, Mennonite Church Canada and several Mennonite educational institutions. Mennonites have also traveled to Iran as part of the friendship and solidarity delegations of the Fellowship of Reconciliation, and Eastern Mennonite University has included Iranian students in its IC3 Foreign Film Series program, in which films are screened at various schools across the world, after which students post their comments and engage in dialogue about the film via the internet. Mennonite individuals from a variety of academic institutions have presented papers at Iranian conferences on human rights, women's, peace, and religious issues. Additionally, the Virginia Mennonite Conference Peace Committee has sponsored an e-pal initiative that connects people in Canada and the United States with Iranians by email. In October 2008, leaders from six Mennonite universities traveled to Iran to meet with officials from twelve Iranian universities to explore possibilities for future collaboration.

II. Things to Keep in Mind When Thinking About Iran

- **Consider current events and issues in their larger contexts.** The items that make the news are only tiny parts of greater historical, cultural, and regional realities that need much study and consideration to be adequately understood. For example, the Iranian revolution can only be understood as we learn about the complex socioeconomic, religious, and historical conditions of the Pahlavi era in which it originated, and Iranian positions on the nuclear issue become more comprehensible when we learn about the history of nuclear development dating back to pre-revolutionary Iranian cooperation with the United States. Likewise, understanding the ways in which imperialism has historically affected Iran sheds light on current-day tensions between Iran and countries in the West.

- **Recognize that both Iranians and North Americans have grievances that need to be addressed.** When thinking about Iran, our own concerns often come to mind first, whether they are related to the hostage crisis, Iran's nuclear program, its human rights record, relationship with Hezbollah, or stance toward Israel. We should keep in mind, however, that from their perspective Iranians have an array of legitimate grievances that deserve to be addressed. These grievances are wide in scope and include the imperialist policies of European governments in the nineteenth and twentieth centuries, United States' involvement in the 1953 coup and support of the Pahlavi regime, the world's support of Iraq in the Iran-Iraq war, and the shooting down of an Iranian commercial airliner. Iranians also call the United States' strong support of Israel misguided and a contributing factor to strife in the Middle East.

- **Remember that our concerns and those of Iranians often overlap, but are not always the same.** Where westerners might be concerned about Iran using its nuclear energy program to develop weapons of mass destruction, many Iranians are worried about rising fuel costs and the inevitable

(continued on next page)

Prophet, who were always keen to achieve their noble goals through the most peaceful ways, even when dealing with their most staunch adversaries. So when I found myself among Mennonites for whom peace is an inviolable principle, I realized I was in the right place.

It did not take long for me to see that my dialogue partners' love for peace was genuine, but I always wondered if these sincere peace-loving people believed that my love for peace was as genuine as theirs. What doubts they might have had were probably rooted, to a large extent, in the way Islam and Iran are pictured in the western media. Yet it also became quickly apparent to both of us that there is a significant difference between the Mennonite pacifist understanding of peace and my Shi'a understanding of it, and that this difference hindered mutual understanding. However, my Mennonite friends and I soon learned that the ability to recognize the differences, no matter how radical they are, is a prerequisite to a successful dialogue. With this appreciation, we have been able to conduct a fruitful dialogue through which we have learned a lot about each other.

Through this learning experience we have managed to cast away the wrong stereotypes we had about each other. Due to my involvement in this dialogue, I have been able to see more clearly than ever the distinction between Christianity and the secular West. During my years as part of the student exchange, I have come to believe that Muslims need to appreciate

(continued on next page)

running out of the petroleum resources on which their economy depends. Similarly, while many in the West are vocal in their criticism of Iran's limited social freedoms, Iranians find themselves concerned by high unemployment rates and a stagnant economy. While western media reports dwell on President Ahmadinejad's comments regarding the Holocaust, the Iranian media focus on the suffering of the Palestinians. These examples are overly general, but they illustrate the fact that our priorities in regards to Iran are not always shared by Iranians themselves, and it is appropriate to prioritize Iranians' concerns when discussing issues related to their country.

- **Recognize that the information we receive about Iran often lacks nuance and is biased or narrow in its concerns.** The brevity of mainstream news reports does not allow for extensive background information or nuanced treatment of the event being reported. In addition, western journalists often rely heavily on Iranian sources most accessible to them, meaning that the grievances of cosmopolitan, western-oriented Iranians get ample air time, while the concerns of middle class, poor, and conservative Iranians often remain unheard. News reports also tend to dwell on negative events, while positive changes go unreported. Thus the potential for misperception and misunderstanding is high. Our perceptions of Iran are also shaped by large communities of Iranians living in the West after fleeing their country in the aftermath of the Islamic Revolution. Iranians living in the West can offer valuable insight into their country of origin, but their experiences and opinions may in some cases differ markedly from those of many Iranians still living inside Iran.

- **Recognize the diversity of Iranian society.** When considering Iran it is important to remember that Iranians are religiously and culturally diverse. The experiences and opinions of an Armenian Christian Iranian living in northeastern Iran, a Shi'a cleric in the seminaries of Qom, and a Sunni Iranian living in a village along the Pakistani border are likely to differ dramatically. Even within specific religious, ethnic, and economic groupings points of view vary, just as they do in our own countries. Any helpful discussion of Iran will take this diversity into account and seek to learn from it.

- **Recognize and respect the differences of opinion that exist on important issues**. As we learn about Iran and dialogue with Iranians, we will find many issues on which we are in agreement. However, we are bound to find differences of opinion as well. Iranian conceptions of human rights may at times differ from our own, as may opinions on the role of religion in government. Likewise, Christian and Islamic teachings differ fundamentally in some respects. Depending upon our perspective and goals we might be tempted either to magnify or trivialize these differences, but a far more helpful path is to recognize them for what they are and maintain respect and kindness in the midst of disagreement.

- **Recognize our own assumptions and the ways in which they differ from those of Iranians.** Our thinking about Iran is often informed by assumptions that Iranians do not share. For example, our focus on Iran's nuclear program is often accompanied by the assumption that the formidable nuclear arsenal of the United States as well as the nuclear weapons capability of other countries in the region including Israel, Pakistan and India are of less concern than Iran's fledgling nuclear energy capacities. Recognizing our assumptions and the reasons why Iranians may not share them will give us a better understanding of contentious issues.

this distinction in their interactions with Christians and Christians need to make this clear to the Muslims with whom they have contact. It has also been helpful that at least some of my Christian dialogue partners have come to see that they should not found their theology of dialogue with Muslims in expressions like "love your enemy," since Muslims are not their enemies. As a matter of fact they can build an intimate friendship with Muslims.

Through our dialogue not only have we come to know each other better, but we have also gained a deeper and more accurate understanding of our own faiths. A good example of this was when I was compelled, due to being part of the exchange, to build my own theology of dialogue. For this purpose, I had to go through the verses that I had spoken many times during my regular recitation of the Qur'an. The first verses that caught my attention were these:

Say: 'People of the Book, let us come to an agreement: that we will worship none but God, that we will associate none with Him, and that none of us shall set up mortals as deities besides God.' If they turn away, say: 'Bear witness, then, that we submit to God.' (3:63-64)

Be courteous when you argue with the People of the Book, except with those among them who do evil. Say: 'We believe in that which has been revealed to us and which was revealed to you Our God and your God is one. To Him we submit.' (29:46)

Prior to that time I had never contemplated and appreciated the congenial tone of these and some other verses. Instead, my attention

(continued on next page)

had mostly been attracted to the criticisms raised by the Qur'an of some creeds and deeds of Christians. It was the first time that I understood that the Qur'an encourages Muslims to engage in dialogue with People of the Book. Later on, I hit upon this fact: usually, when the Qur'an gives Muslims advice about how to talk to People of the Book, it mostly recommends that we concentrate on what is common between us, while almost all the grievances of the Qur'an against People of the Book occur in the context of God talking directly about or to them.

It is worth mentioning that all this has been achieved because we could place our dialogue in a context of friendship. Dialogue between religions, in my view, is not an academic task that can be conducted merely by exchanging words and concepts. Instead, dialogue between religions is a meeting of hearts seeking the truths that belong first and foremost within hearts. Such a task is fruitful only if the hearts of those who dialogue are connected to one another by the thread of friendship. That such friendship was established soon after our arrival in Canada should be credited mostly to the warm hospitality of our Mennonite hosts. I am thankful to all of them, who are too many to name. However, I feel compelled to name and thank Mr. Ed Martin, Ms. Susan Harrison, and Dr. James Reimer. My appreciation for the role they played in this exchange with their kind hearts and hard work is too great to express in words.

- **Recognize the common interests of our countries.** Issues of dispute between Iran and western nations have been loudly broadcast by the media. As a result, many do not realize that both sides have common interests. Iran and the United States, for all their mutual animosity, both have an interest in the return of peace and stability to Iraq and Afghanistan, and meetings between the two parties to facilitate this end have been at least somewhat productive. Curbing the traffic of narcotics from Afghanistan is another common goal. Recognizing these and other common interests and working together to achieve mutually beneficial goals can pave the way toward the resolution of disputes.

- **Explore the potential for friendship and learning between the people of Iran, Canada, and the United States.** With much of the West's interest in Iran focusing on issues of political dispute, it is easy to forget that Iran is a treasure trove of cultural and religious resources from which we have much to learn. Many academic, religious, cultural, charitable, and other types of organizations have expressed interest in partnerships with western institutions and individuals, and such cooperation has the potential to forge rich friendships between societies that have relatively little contact.

III. Working for Peace: What Can We Do?

PRAY

Among other prayers, we can pray:

- For a just, nonviolent resolution to the tensions between Iran and the United States as well as other countries. Pray that government officials will be open to comprehensive negotiations and creative solutions to problems.

- For just, peaceful resolutions to the conflicts in Afghanistan, Iraq, and Palestine-Israel, all of which have a tremendous destabilizing effect on the Middle East region and beyond.

- That Muslims and Christians will live together in harmony and cultivate an attitude of mutual respect. Pray particularly for Christian minorities in the Middle East and Muslim minorities in Europe, Canada, and the United States.

- For improvements in the economic situation in Iran and solutions to other problems faced by the country.

LEARN

Most people living in Canada and the United States know little about Iran, and acquiring basic knowledge about the people, history, religions, and cultures of that country can break down common stereotypes and fears, ease tension, and foster a climate of respect. Often the most gratifying approach is to investigate areas of personal interest. Some may find themselves interested in Iranian politics and current events, while others may find pleasure in exploring Iranian history, literature, or cinema. Still others may be curious about Shi'a Islam or enjoy learning about the histories of minority religions in Iran. When possible, however, the best way to learn about Iran is by getting to know Iranians. Check to see if an Iranian/Persian cultural society exists in your area and has events you can attend, or contact MCC to see if participants in its Iran exchange program might be visiting your area. Consider joining one of MCC's learning tours to Iran, which give participants a first-hand experience of the country and its people.

GIVE

Contribute time or money to organizations whose goal it is to promote just and peaceful relations with Iran. Information on MCC's Iran program can be found at **http://www.mcc.org/iran**.

Top: : Members of an MCC learning tour beside a pair of giant boots, all that remains of a statue of Reza Shah at Niyavaran Palace in Tehran.

Bottom: Ron Flaming, MCC's director of international programs, sits with former Iranian president Muhammad Khatami in a meeting that took place during the 2007 visit of U.S. religious leaders to Iran.

A doorway in Esfahan.

ADVOCATE

Advocacy personnel in MCC's Ottawa, United Nations, and Washington D.C. offices (**http://www.mcc.org/advocacy**) have been working toward peace on issues pertaining to Iran for some time. Of particular concern in 2008 was persistent talk of military action by Israel or the United States against Iran. Citizens of the United States can work to change their country's foreign policy toward Iran and the Middle East by contacting their government representatives. Encourage your representatives to support comprehensive negotiations without preconditions between Iran and the United States, and express opposition to negative legislation that increases sanctions or paves the way for military actions against Iran. In the non-governmental sphere, you can help build peace by increasing awareness of current events and issues related to Iran in your church or broader community as well as encouraging those around you to learn about Iran and Islam.

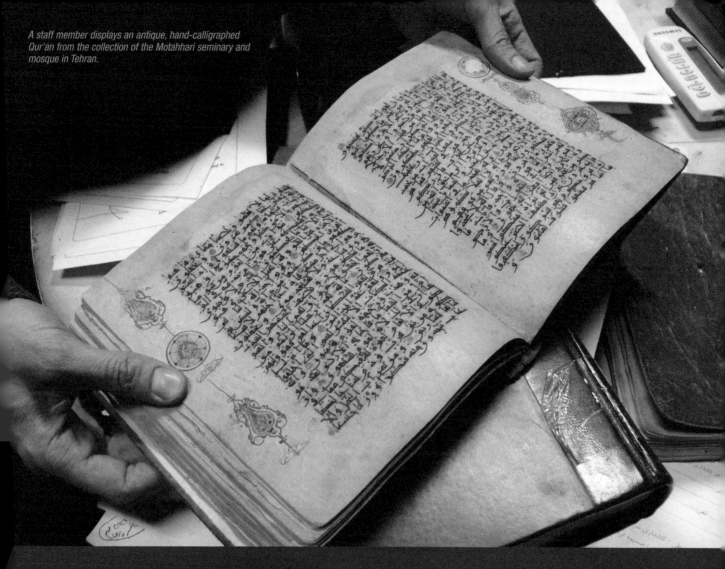

A staff member displays an antique, hand-calligraphed Qur'an from the collection of the Motahhari seminary and mosque in Tehran.

Resources for Further Study

Iranian sightseers take photographs at the ruins of Persepolis.

Resources for Further Study

I. Iran

GENERAL

A History of Iran: Empire of the Mind, by Michael Axworthy (New York: Basic Books, 2008): An overview of Iran from ancient times to the present.

Iran's Diverse Peoples: A Reference Sourcebook, by Massoume Price (Santa Barbara, CA: ABC Clio, 2005): A book that traces the origins and histories of the diverse peoples of Iran.

Iran Chamber Society (http://www.iranchamber.com/): An internet resource for information on the history and culture of Iran.

CIA World Factbook (https://www.cia.gov/library/publications/the-world-factbook/geos/ir.html): Brief overviews and statistics on many facets of life in Iran.

HISTORY, POLITICS AND SOCIETY IN THE 20TH CENTURY AND BEYOND

In the Rose Garden of the Martyrs: A Memoir of Iran, by Christopher de Bellaigue (New York: HarperCollins, 2004): An account of the author's life in Iran, interspersed with information on Iranian history and society in the revolutionary period and beyond.

Iran Awakening: One Woman's Journey to Reclaim Her Life and Country, by Shirin Ebadi and Azadeh Moaveni (New York: Random House, 2007): The memoir of Nobel Prize-winning Iranian human rights activist Shirin Ebadi.

Takeover in Tehran: The Inside Story of the 1979 U.S. Embassy Capture, by Massoumeh Ebtekar and Fred Reed (Vancouver, BC: Talonbooks, 2000): The Iranian woman who served as a translator between the media and the captives tells the story of the hostage crisis from an Iranian perspective. Ebtekar, who went on to serve as Iran's first female vice president, is the director of an NGO and keeps a blog at http://ebtekarm.blogspot.com/.

Iran Today: An Encyclopedia of Life in the Islamic Republic, edited by Mehran Kamrava and Manochehr Dorraj (Westport, CT: Greenwood Press, 2008): A two-volume work with useful, up-to-date information on history, politics, economics, society and culture in Iran.

Modern Iran: Roots and Results of Revolution, by Nikkie Keddie (New Haven, CT: Yale University Press, 2006): The updated edition of a work that traces history, politics, society, and culture from the Qajar period to the present time.

Mantle of the Prophet, by Roy Mottahedeh (New York: Simon and Schuster, 1985): An enjoyable and informative account of the Iranian revolution that alternates between historical narrative and the fictionalized biography of a Shi'a cleric's experience of the events described.

Khomeini: Life of the Ayatollah, by Baqer Moin (London: I. B. Taurus, 1999): A detailed biography of Khomeini that explains forces influencing his thought, faith and action.

Treacherous Alliance: The Secret Dealings of Israel, Iran and the U.S., by Trita Parsi (New Haven, CT: Yale University Press, 2007): An examination of relations among the United States, Iran, and Israel from 1948 to the present.

Amnesty International (http://thereport.amnesty.org/eng/regions/middle-east-and-north-africa/iran): Online version of the Amnesty International 2008 report on the status of human rights in Iran.

International Atomic Energy Agency (http://www.iaea.org/NewsCenter/Focus/Iaea Iran/): The IAEA webpage on Iran contains detailed reports of Iran's nuclear program since 2003.

MINORITY FAITHS

Religious Minorities in Iran, by Eliz Sanasarian, (Cambridge, UK: Cambridge University Press, 2000): An overview of religious minorities from 1979 to 2000.

A History of Christianity in Asia, by Samuel Hugh Moffett (Maryknoll, NY: Orbis Books, 1998 and 2005): A three-volume work on the history of Christianity in Asia, including Iran. Volume one covers the period from the beginning of Christianity to 1500, while the second volume covers the years between 1500 and 1900. The third volume is in progress.

Esther's Children: A Portrait of Iranian Jews, Houman Sarshar, ed., (Beverly Hills, CA: Center for Iranian Jewish Oral History, 2002): A beautifully illustrated book chronicling over two thousand years of history of the Jewish community in Iran.

Tehran Jewish Association (http://www.iranjewish.com/): The official website of the Jewish community in Tehran.

The Baha'i Faith (http://www.bahai.org/): The official website of the Baha'i international community.

THE ARTS

I Heard God Laughing: Poems of Hope and Joy, by Hafiz, trans. by Daniel Ladinsky (New York: Penguin, 2008): Poems of famous Persian writer Hafiz in loose translation.

The Essential Rumi, by Jelaluddin Rumi, trans. by Coleman Barks (San Francisco: Harper San Francisco, 1995): Poems of the famous poet and mystic in loose translation.

Stories from Iran: An Anthology of Persian Short Fiction from 1921–1991, Heshmat Moayyad, ed. (Washington, DC: Mage Publishers, 1991): Translations of some of the most famous short fiction by Iranian authors of the twentieth century.

A Persian Requiem, by Simin Daneshvar, trans. by Roxanne Zand (New York: George Braziller, 1992): English translation of what is arguably the most famous novel by an Iranian author.

Children of Heaven, Dir. Majid Majidi; Perfs. Mohammad Amir Naji, Amir Farrokh Hashemian (Miramax, 2002): Beautiful and uplifting Iranian film exploring family relationships and the essence of childhood, subtitled in English and French.

Taste of Cherry, Dir. Abbas Kiarostami; Perfs. Homayon Ershadi, Abdolrahman Bagheri (Criterion, 1999): Persian film that won the *Palme d'Or*, subtitled in English.

II. Islam

GENERAL

Islam: An Introduction, by Annemarie Schimmel (Albany, NY: State University of New York Press, 1992): A brief and readable presentation of Islam by an outstanding scholar of Islam, Sufism, and Persian Literature.

Islam: Religion, History and Civilization, by Seyyed Hossein Nasr (San Francisco: Harper San Francisco, 2003): An overview of Islam by a noted Shi'a cleric and scholar.

The Call of the Minaret, by Kenneth Cragg (Oxford: Oneworld Publications, 2000): An overview of Islam by a Christian theologian who offers advice on how Christians can relate helpfully to Islam.

Islam: Past, Present, and Future, by Hans Kung (Oxford: Oneworld Publications, 2007): The third of a series in which the famous Christian theologian critically examines the Abrahamic faiths.

Women and Gender in Islam, by Leila Ahmed (New Haven, CT: Yale University Press, 1992): Premier work on the topic in English by noted Muslim feminist.

SHI'A ISLAM

Shi'ite Anthology, edited and translated by William Chittick (Albany, NY: SUNY Press, 1981): A collection of well-known Shi'a writings.

Expectation of the Millenium: Shi'ism in History, edited by Seyyed Hossein Nasr, Seyyed Vali Reza Nasr and Hamid Dabashi (Albany, NY: SUNY Press, 1989): Noted academics and religious scholars contributed to this work detailing the history of Shi'a Islam.

Shi'i Islam: Origins, Faith & Practices, by Mohammad A. Shomali (London: Islamic College for Advanced Studies, 2003): An overview of Shi'a Islam by a Shi'a cleric who has worked extensively in Christian-Muslim relations.

Doctrines of Shi'i Islam: A Compendium of Imami Beliefs and Practices, by Ayatollah Jafar Sobhani, translated by Reza Shah-Kazemi (London: I. B. Tauris, 2001): An overview of Shi'a theology and jurisprudence.

Al-Islam.org (http://www.al-islam.org/): A website containing a variety of resources about Shi'a Islam.

III. Mennonite Resources

Mennonite Central Committee (http://mcc.org/)

Mennonite Central Committee in Iran (http://mcc.org/iran/)

Iran Exchange. MCC Peace Office Newsletter, 31(3). July-September 2001: http://mcc.org/peace/pon/PON_2001-03.pdf

Interfaith Bridge Building. MCC Peace Office Newsletter, 35(4). October-December 2005: http://mcc.org/peace/pon/PON_2005-04.pdf

Christians and Muslims Reflecting Together. MCC Peace Office Newsletter, 36(1). January-March 2006: http://mcc.org/peace/pon/PON_2006-01.pdf

Iran: Visits and Dialogue. MCC Peace Office Newsletter, 37(3). July-September 2007: http://mcc.org/peace/pon/PON_2007-03.pdf

The Challenge of Modernity. The *Conrad Grebel Review*, 21(3). Fall 2003: An issue of the review containing a collection of papers from the first Mennonite-Shi'a dialogue conference held in Canada in 2002.

Revelation and Authority. The *Conrad Grebel Review*, 24(1). Winter 2006: An issue of the review containing four papers presented in the second Mennonite-Shi'a dialogue conference, held in Iran in 2004.

Anabaptists Meeting Muslims: A Calling for Presence in the Way of Christ, eds. James R. Krabill, David W. Shenk, and Linford Stutzman (Scottdale, PA: Herald Press, 2004): Essays and reports from Anabaptists in relationships with Muslims around the world.

Perspectives on Mennonite-Shi'a Dialogue. Anabaptist-Mennonite Scholars Network Newsletter, 11(2). Fall 2008: http://www.anabaptistscholars.net/2008fall.pdf. This newsletter contains three articles written by Mennonite scholars who have participated in MCC involvement with Iran.

What is Palestine-Israel? Answers to Common Questions, by Sonia K. Weaver (Scottdale, PA: Herald Press, 2007): An overview of the Palestinian-Israeli conflict rooted in MCC experience in the region.

The Author

Laurie Blanton Pierce has an abiding interest in Islam, Iran, and Persian language and literature birthed out of a decade of living in the Middle East and South Asia. In 2006 she returned to her home country of the United States after studying for three years in Iran as part of Mennonite Central Committee's Muslim-Christian exchange program. She lives with her husband and two children in Boston, where she works as a freelance editor and writer.